THE POCKET DARING BOOK FOR GIRLS:

DISCOVERIES & PASTIMES

Praise for *The Daring Book for Girls*

'Gung-ho girly advice . . . the boys had their Dangerous book, now this one is for us'   *Good Housekeeping*

'I can't imagine not wanting to get stuck in to *The Daring Book for Girls*. It's an admirable project'
                                        Jenny Diski, *Sunday Times*

'The authors mix inspiring tales of girls who made good . . . with a scrap bag of how-tos for girlish activities . . . *The Daring Book for Girls* keeps . . . practical knowledge from getting drowned in the techno-flow'   *The New York Times*

'We've had The Dangerous Book for Boys – now it's our turn. Refreshingly, it's not about lipstick tips, but pioneering women who inspire us'   *Glamour*

THE POCKET DARING BOOK FOR GIRLS:

DISCOVERIES & PASTIMES

This book mixes much-loved chapters from the popular *The Daring Book for Girls* with even more stories and fun facts. Perfect for girls on the go, this portable and pocket-sized book of Discoveries and Pastimes is just the thing for anyone who loves to discover new ideas and trade newfound knowledge with family and friends. It's the perfect companion for the adventures that come your way, and for the moments between them.

Daring Girl badges and other downloads available at
www.daringbookforgirls.com

HarperCollins*Publishers*

HarperCollins*Publishers*
77–85 Fulham Palace Road,
Hammersmith, London W6 8JB

www.harpercollins.co.uk

Published by HarperCollins*Publishers* 2008
1

First published in the US, in a slightly different edition
by HarperCollins*Publishers* 2008

A catalogue record for this book
is available from the British Library

ISBN: 978–0–00–728989–9

Set in Minion by Newgen Imaging Systems (P) Ltd, Chennai, India

Printed and bound in Italy by L.E.G.O. SpA – Vicenza

NOTE TO PARENTS: This book contains a number of activities that may be dangerous if
not done exactly as directed or that may be inappropriate for young children. All of these
activities should be carried out under adult supervision only. The authors and publishers
expressly disclaim liability for any injury or damages that result from engaging in
the activities contained in this book.

Andrea Buchanan and Miriam Peskowitz

The Pocket

DARING

Book
for

Girls

Discoveries & Pastimes

HarperCollins*Publishers*

CONTENTS

———————◆———————

INTRODUCTION

W E THINK 'Did you know?' is a wonderfully world-opening question, ripe with discovery and possibility. To build this pocket version of *The Daring Book for Girls*, we took the phrase seriously – and had lots of fun with it. To our favourite queens, pirates and pilots from the original *Daring Book for Girls* we added a slew of interesting stories, from curiosities about tongue twisters, to haiku, layers of the earth and air and elliptical galaxies. We also tossed in some facts about Doric columns, the history of zero and the mysterious Fibonacci numbers.

True daring is all about enjoying yourself, exploring new things and leading an interesting life. We hope this collection of Discoveries and Pastimes spurs you on that journey.

Andrea Buchanan

Miriam Peskowitz

THE DARING GIRL'S GUIDE
TO DANGER

❖

FACING YOUR FEARS can be a rewarding experience and pushing yourself to new heights will inspire you to face challenges throughout life. Here in no particular order is a checklist of danger and daring. Some you should be able to do right away, but a few you might need to work up to:

1 **Ride a roller coaster.** The tallest roller coaster in the UK is Oblivion at Alton Towers in Staffordshire with a terrifying near vertical drop of over 50 metres. The Colossus at Thorpe Park, Chertsey, has the greatest number of rolls in the country, looping the loop ten times during the ride. And the longest roller coaster in the UK is the Ultimate at Lightwater Valley near Ripon – it's nearly one and a half miles long and takes five minutes to complete.

2 **Ride a zip line across the canopy of a rainforest.** A trip to Costa Rica offers incredible adventures, including 'flying' across the roof of the world 60 metres off the ground with distances between trees of up to 360 metres. Many outdoor centres around the UK also offer zip line courses.

3 **Go white-water rafting.** Most people think looking at the Grand Canyon from the rim down is scary, but a true act of daring is to take a white-water rafting trip down the stretch of Colorado River that cuts through it. Some trips even include a helicopter ride for an extra dose of danger!

4 **Have a scary movie festival in your living room.** Some good ones are *The Exorcist, Jaws, Alien, The Shining* and Alfred Hitchcock's classic but still frightening *Psycho*. But don't blame us if you can't go to sleep without wondering what's under the bed.

5 **Wear high heels.** This may not sound so dangerous, but without practice you can fall or twist an ankle. For your first time in heels, borrow someone else's and make sure to start on a hard surface like wood. Once you're feeling steady on your feet, give carpeting a try. If you can wear heels on a thick carpet, you can do anything. Eventually, if it's a skill you want to learn, you'll be able to run, jump and do karate in three-inch heels.

6 **Stand up for yourself – or someone else.** It's scary to feel like you're the only one who doesn't agree, but when

something's wrong, a daring girl speaks up, for herself or someone who needs an ally. Summon your courage and raise your voice – real bravery is feeling the fear and doing it anyway.

7 **Try sushi or another exotic food.** Rice in seaweed does not count. For the true daring girl try some *natto* (fermented soya beans) or *escargots* (snails).

8 **Dye your hair purple.** Sometimes the scariest thing is just being a little bit different, even for a day. There are many hair dyes that wash out after a few weeks – so you can experience what it would be like to have a lime-green ponytail without having to wait for all your hair to grow out to change it again.

WOMEN WHO CHANGED
THE WORLD

◆

Jane Goodall (b. 1934)

JANE GOODALL WAS born in London. Always fascinated by animals, she was the sort of girl who wanted to get really close to them and truly understand their nature. She once hid inside a henhouse for hours, just to discover how hens were able to lay eggs. Little did she realize that outside her hiding place all chaos was unleashed as her parents frantically searched for her!

So, when a friend invited her to visit her at her family farm in Kenya, Jane jumped at the chance. She knew that there she would see animals that she could only dream of at home in England. Once in Kenya she met palaeontologist and anthropologist Dr Louis Leakey who was looking for someone to go to the Gombe Stream National Park in Tanzania to study wild chimpanzees. He saw the enthusiasm that Jane had for animals and decided that she would be an ideal candidate.

This was the turning point of Jane's life. It was unheard of for a woman to go into the African jungle alone so, accompanied by her mother, Jane, aged only twenty-three, took off for the adventure of a lifetime. What she discovered in Gombe would revolutionize science.

Once in the jungle, she realized that chimpanzees formed relationships with each other, had affection for each other and even seemed to assist each other purely for the sake of helping, rather than for any reward. But what was most crucial was her understanding of the way in which chimpanzees used tools to help them fish termites out of a termite mound. They were the only animals, aside from humans, to use tools in this way. It was a remarkable discovery.

Jane has carried her work into the wider world by founding the Jane Goodall Institute for Wildlife Research, Education and Conservation. Originally set up to support projects like her own, observing wild chimpanzees, it now educates people about the environment and the importance of protecting it for both animals and humans. She's a remarkable woman whose life is an inspiration to girls everywhere. The little girl who once crawled into a henhouse is still travelling, still learning, still telling stories about how the world works, and still helping others to protect it.

FRENCH TERMS

Numbers

0	zéro	11	onze
1	un	12	douze
2	deux	13	treize
3	trois	14	quatorze
4	quatre	15	quinze
5	cinq	16	seize
6	six	17	dix-sept
7	sept	18	dix-huit
8	huit	19	dix-neuf
9	neuf	20	vingt
10	dix	100	cent

Fun things to say

Mon frère	my brother (for sibling and friend)
Ma soeur	my sister (for sibling and friend)
Ouille! Aïe!	Ouch! (pronounced Oo-y! Ah-ee!)
Zut! Or *Zut alors!*	An expression of surprise (like 'Darn it!')
J'ai la pêche!	Literally 'I've got the peach!' Full of energy and ready to go. (You can also say *J'ai la patate, J'ai la banane, J'ai la frite* – I've got the potato, I've got the banana, I've got the chips!)

Tongue Twisters (Les Virelangues)

Les chaussettes de l'archiduchesse sont-elles sèches? Archi-sèches!	'The archduchess's socks are dry, extra dry!'
Un chasseur sachant chasser doit savoir chasser sans son chien.	'A hunter knowing how to hunt has to know how to hunt without his [hunting] dog.'

Si ces six-cent saucissons-ci sont six-cent sous, ces six-cent-six saucissons-là sont six-cent-six sous.	'If these 600 salamis cost 600 pennies, those 606 salamis cost 606 pennies.'
Je veux et j'exige d'exquises excuses.	'I want and I demand delightful apologies.'

Food

Frites	Chips
Pâtes au gruyère	Macaroni cheese
Crème au chocolat	Chocolate pudding
Flan au caramel	Crème caramel
Yaourts à boire	Drinkable yogurt
Fondant au chocolat	Small chocolate cake with warm, melting insides
Tarte sablée au citron	Lemon pie with a tender, buttery crust

Travel and Adventure

Où est la gare routière?	Where is the bus station?
Quand part le prochain bateau pour Tunis et combien coûte le voyage?	When is the next boat to Tunis, and how much does the fare cost?
Devons nous visiter le Comoros pour voir le volcan du Mont Karthala?	Shall we visit the Comoros to see the volcano at Mount Karthala?

Did You Know? French-Speaking Countries

Bien sur (of course!), French is the primary language of France. But did you know that it is also an official language of more than fifty-five francophone nations and regions around the globe? Among these are the Democratic Republic of the Congo, Canada, Madagascar, Côte d'Ivoire, Cameroon, Burkina Faso, Niger, Senegal, Mali, Belgium, Chad, Guinea, Rwanda, Haiti, Burundi, Benin, Switzerland, Togo, Central African Republic, Lebanon, Republic of the Congo, Gabon, Comoros, Equatorial Guinea, Djibouti, Luxembourg, Vanuatu, Seychelles, Monaco and more.

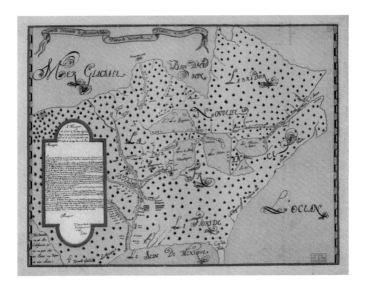

French is spoken in the Arabic-speaking North African countries of Morocco, Algeria, Tunisia and Mauritania, a reflection of their former status as French-occupied colonies. In Senegal, another former colony, French is spoken alongside native languages like Wolof, Pulaar, Jola and Mandinka.

Fun Fact: North Africa is sometimes called the Maghreb, which in Arabic means the place of sunset, or 'the west'. The Maghreb is divided from the rest of Africa by the Atlas Mountains and by the Sahara desert.

Fun Fact: With over one billion speakers, the most-spoken language on earth is Mandarin Chinese. The list of other top-spoken world languages also includes English, Hindi-Urdu and the other languages of India; Spanish; Russian; Arabic; Bengali; Portuguese and the Malay languages of Indonesia and French.

Although in the majority Canada is English-speaking, the province of Québec is francophone, and it protects its French heritage fiercely. The capital is Québec City, and it was settled by French explorers and soldiers and fur traders in 1608, making it one of North America's oldest cities. The name sounds French, but it actually comes from an Algonquin word, *kebec* which means 'where the river narrows'.

Cajun French is still spoken in Louisiana. In the 1680s, the French explorer René-Robert de la Salle sailed southward down the Mississippi River. He named the region 'Louisiana' after the powerful French king Louis XIV. French-speaking settlers arrived soon after from Acadia, which is the area around Nova Scotia, and they brought French with them. Sometimes Cajun is confused with Creole, another Louisiana language which is a mixture of native, African, Caribbean and Western European language.

Fun Fact: De la Salle's ship *La Belle* sunk in Matagorda Bay, off the coast of Texas, and was discovered by archaeologists in 1995.

Few people know that in Wisconsin there's a French-Belgian dialect called Walloon. In the nineteenth century, people left Wallonia, the French-speaking part of Belgium south of Brussels, and settled on the Wisconsin peninsula that sits between Green Bay and Lake Michigan. They brought the French-Belgian dialect of Walloon with them and even today in Wisconsin as in southern Belgium, you can hear phrases like *Bondjoû* (Hello) and *Arvey* (Goodbye), and *Cmint daloz?* (How are you?).

RULES OF THE GAME: ROUNDERS

---◆---

ROUNDERS IS AN important part of every girl's school life. If she's lucky she'll continue to play it later in life. It has always been popular in the UK, with the first recorded game being played in Tudor times. Jane Austen, the grand-dame of all things English and female, even mentions it in *Northanger Abbey*, so all Austen fans really *ought* to know how to play rounders! And anyway, it's a great way to spend an afternoon in the park with some friends, and that should always be encouraged.

SOME THINGS TO KNOW

Rounders is played by two teams of between six and fifteen players, organized into batters and fielders.

The only equipment you need is a long, thin, round bat (although often we play with a cricket bat, and even sometimes a tennis racket – Miss Austen would be horrified!) and a small round ball (again, any ball will do if you don't have the proper rounders ball).

The pitch is made up of four bases, a bowling area and a batting area. Bases are traditionally poles which are placed in the ground but you can improvise, using long sticks or whatever you have to hand.

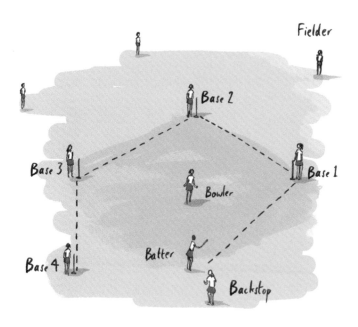

Batters have two 'good' balls (or 'innings') per game and the aim is to hit the ball as best they can and successfully run around the four bases on the pitch without being stumped or caught out. If you are stumped, you're out. Once the ball is returned to the bowler, you must stop at the base you are on and may not move again until the next ball is bowled to the next batter.

Fielders must aim to either catch the batter out or catch the ball and throw it to one of the fielders near the bases to touch the base before the running batter can reach it.

RULES OF THE GAME

A 'good' ball must be thrown underarm, aiming for the batter's striking side, between the knees and the shoulders. It should not hit the ground before it reaches the batter.

Once the batter has hit the ball, she must run around the bases aiming to reach fourth base before the ball is returned to the bowler and she must stop running.

A rounder (another name for a point) is scored if the batter manages to reach fourth base without being 'out'.

You can be out if a fielder catches the ball after you have hit it, or if a fielder 'stumps' the base you are running to before you can reach it. Once you are out you must sit out and you cannot score a rounder in that game.

Two innings make up a game, and each team can continue either until all their players are out or each player has played both of their innings. The team with the most rounders wins.

JOAN OF ARC

❖

'One life is all we have and we live it as we believe in living it. But to sacrifice what you are and to live without belief, that is a fate more terrible than dying.'

Joan of Arc

JOAN WAS BORN around 1412 in the small town of Domrémy in France, on the border of the provinces of Champagne and Lorraine, to Jacques d'Arc and Isabelle Romée. She grew up helping her father and brothers work the land and helping her mother, a devout woman, look after the house.

The year she turned twelve, she became convinced that there was something special about her – a destiny she alone could fulfil. She began hearing the voices of St Michael, St Catherine and St Margaret, whom she believed had been sent by God to inform her of her divine mission to save France. So compelled was she by the urgency of these voices that by the time she was fifteen she cut her hair, began dressing in a man's uniform and took up arms.

France and England were deep into the Hundred Years War at this point. At that time in history, the two nations were not as separate as they are now and there was a battle raging over who should be king of the general area. By 1429, King Henry VI was claiming the throne and the English occupied Paris and all of northern France. Joan had two missions, thanks to the voices that guided her: to recover her homeland from English domination and reclaim the besieged city of Orléans; and to see the dauphin of France, Charles VII, crowned king. She left her home, without telling her parents, and appealed to the captain of the dauphin's army, telling him of her divine mission. He initially dismissed the notion of a fifteen-year-old girl having the leadership capacity to head his forces. However, her persistence and clarity of vision ultimately convinced him, and she went on to convince the dauphin as well that she was on a mission from God meant to save him and restore France. After being examined by a board of theologians, she was given the rank of captain and allowed to lead men into battle.

She was seventeen when she led her troops to victory over the English at the battle of Orléans in May 1429. She rode in white armour and carried a banner bearing the likenesses of her three saints. It wasn't all that unusual at that time for women to fight alongside men; indeed, throughout the Middle Ages women had, when necessary, worn armour, led armies, ridden horses and defended castles and lands. Joan was an excellent leader. Through her self-assured confidence,

JOAN OF ARC

her courage and her determination, she was able to effectively command soldiers and captains alike. She organized her army of men into professional soldiers and even required them to attend mass and go to confession. So formidable was her leadership that it was said when her troops approached, the enemy fled the battlefield. But by far her most innovative act was instilling among her people a sense of nationalism and patriotic pride: she was one of the first leaders to consider England and France as separate countries, with separate cultures and traditions that were worth fighting to preserve.

Due in great part to Joan's leadership on the battlefield, Charles VII was crowned king of France on 17 July 1429 in Reims Cathedral. Her victory, however, was short-lived: she was captured by the Burgundians in 1430 while defending Compiègne, near Paris, and was sold to the English. The English turned her over to the court at Rouen to be tried for witchcraft and crimes against the church. Though the witchcraft charge was dismissed (on the grounds that she was a virgin), she was accused of perpetrating crimes against God by wearing men's clothing. After a fourteen-month trial, during which she never strayed from her insistence on the divinity of her voices and the absolute rightness of her calling, Joan was convicted and burned at the stake in the Rouen marketplace on 30 May 1431. Her last words were 'Jesus! Jesus!' She was nineteen years old.

Almost twenty-five years after her death, Pope Callixtus III reopened the case at the request of Inquisitor-General Jean Brehal and Joan's mother Isabelle Romée. Joan was vindicated as a martyr and declared an innocent woman on 7 July 1456. It was nearly 500 years after her death that she was canonized as a saint, on 16 May 1920, by Pope Benedict XV. Joan of Arc is now recognized as the patron saint of France.

The story of a girl guided by voices to change the world has proved irresistible to storytellers and artists from the time of her death to the present day. She continues to serve as an inspiration to daring girls everywhere.

GALAXIES

⬥

GALAXIES ARE ENORMOUS, organized systems of stars, star clusters, dust and gas. As vast as it seems to us here on Earth, our galaxy, the Milky Way, is just one of billions of galaxies in the universe. Exactly how many galaxies exist isn't known – there may be as many as 100 billion galaxies in just the part of the universe scientists can actually observe – and scientists also aren't sure about just where galaxies came from and how they were formed. What we do know is that galaxies can contain anywhere from several million to several trillion stars (our own galaxy, the Milky Way, contains somewhere in the neighbourhood of 100 billion stars, including the sun); that they can be separated by as little as few thousands of light years to millions of light years in distance; and that they come in three basic shapes: spiral, elliptical and irregular.

Spiral

Our Milky Way galaxy is a spiral galaxy, its twisting, whorling shape resembling water circling around a drain, a hurricane as seen from a satellite or a child's pinwheel blowing in the breeze.

Spiral galaxies usually have an 'eye' at the centre (a disk with a bulging centre made up of stars, planets, dust and gas) and spiralling arms extending outward in a spinning motion. Everything rotates around the galactic centre at speeds of hundreds of kilometres per second. A faster or slower rotation can affect a galaxy's shape – such as a kind of spiral galaxy called a 'sombrero galaxy' due to its flattened, spread-out appearance. The bulge at the centre of the galactic disk is where older stars usually reside, while newer stars often form in the galaxy's spiralling arms. The newer stars are often quite large, and very bright, but they don't last very long: their sheer size causes them to burn out quickly. Smaller stars that aren't quite as luminous last longer.

Why is it called the Milky Way?

Our galaxy's nickname, the Milky Way, comes from the Greek *kyklos galaktikos*, or 'milky circle' which likens its appearance in the distant sky to glistening drops of spilled milk. But why milk? Greek mythology tells the interesting tale. In one of the many colourful stories the Greeks used to explain the natural world, Zeus (the king of the gods and the god of thunder) tricked Hera (goddess of women and marriage) into breastfeeding his mortal son Heracles by placing the baby on her breast while she was sleeping. His plan was to have the baby drink Hera's milk and thus become a god like him. But Hera awoke and pushed the baby away, causing the milk to spray across the night sky.

The Milky Way around the world

In the Baltic languages, the Milky Way is called the 'Bird's Path'. In ancient China it was called the 'Heavenly River of Han' and in contemporary China and other parts of Asia it is called 'Silver River'. In Japan, 'Silver River' is used to refer to galaxies in general, while the Milky Way is called the 'Silver River System' or the 'River of Heaven'. In Sweden, the Milky Way is called *Vintergatan* or 'Winter Street'.

The term Milky Way first appeared in the English language in 1380 in a poem by Geoffrey Chaucer titled 'The House of Fame'. (The poem is written in Middle English, which, as you can see in the spelling below, differs from the modern English we use today.)

> *See yonder, lo, the Galaxyë*
> *Which men clepeth the Milky Wey,*
> *For hit is whyt.*

Elliptical

Elliptical galaxies often have an elongated, rugby-ball-like shape. Unlike spiral galaxies they do not have a disk at their centre. Elliptical galaxies are also usually smaller than spiral galaxies and may contain anywhere from a few thousand stars to billions of stars. Most of the stars in an elliptical galaxy are very old and often clustered together, which makes the centre appear as though it is one giant star. It is very rare that new stars form in these types of galaxies. Very large elliptical galaxies, called Giant elliptical galaxies, are the largest galaxies in the universe that we know of and can be as much as two million light years in length.

Galactic measurements

The distances between galaxies are so huge, they are usually measured in astronomical units calls megaparsecs. Just one parsec equals about 19,176,075,967,325 miles. A megaparsec is one million parsecs – which is about 3.3 million light years. So instead of saying that our nearest neighbour, the Andromeda Galaxy (another spiral system), is 2 to 3 million light years from us, we can say that the distance between the Milky Way and the Andromeda Galaxy is about 0.899 megaparsecs.

Irregular

Irregular galaxies are just what they sound like: irregularly shaped galaxies that are neither spiral nor elliptical. They can appear misshapen or formless. This may be due to crashes with other galaxies, or it may be that they have always been shaped that way.

WOMEN WHO CHANGED
THE WORLD

❖

Indira Gandhi (1917–84)

THE INDIA IN which Indira Gandhi (then Nehru, before her marriage to Feroze Gandhi) was born was one of turmoil and unrest. Growing up in the 1920s and 1930s, she was surrounded by politics – her father was an important member of the pro-independence party, the Indian National Congress, which was led by Mahatma Gandhi. Even as a young girl she wanted her country to be independent of Britain and so, determined to help in any way she could, she formed Vanara Sena. Meaning 'Army of Monkeys', Vanara Sena was a group of Indian boys and girls, all committed to independence, who joined together under Indira's leadership to make flags and sing patriotic songs. Indira is said to have used her schoolbag to smuggle out of her father's house a document important to the revolutionaries, right under the noses of the police who kept them under constant surveillance.

When India achieved autonomy from Britain in 1947 and India and Pakistan were formed as new and independent countries, Indira's father, Jawaharlal Nehru, was elected as India's first independent Prime Minister. But the creation of

WOMEN WHO CHANGED THE WORLD: INDIRA GANDHI

India and Pakistan resulted in the immediate migration of hundreds of thousands of people as Hindus and Sikhs moved to India from Pakistan and Muslims moved from India to Pakistan, all seeking safety among others of their own religion. Indira flew into action and organized refugee camps for the dispossessed, providing shelter and medical aid. This experience gave her confidence that she too might one day become a great political leader.

It would take nearly twenty years, but she achieved her goal and became the first female Prime Minister of India in 1966. As a leader, she relied on the populist vote. Campaigning on an anti-poverty ticket, she focused on agricultural reform that would ensure that the people had at least enough to eat. But she was also accused of being dictatorial, ruthlessly suppressing dissent. She called elections in 1977 but lost and was forced from power and arrested on corruption charges. Determined to get back what she saw as her rightful position, she stood again at elections in 1979 and won in a landslide victory. Despite this success, her later years were darkened with violence and unrest as Sikh separatists fought for independence in the Punjab. She ordered their leaders to be killed in a bloody battle in one of Sikhism's holiest shrines, the Golden Temple. This would prove to be a fatal mistake. In October 1984 two men, her own bodyguards, assassinated her in the gardens of her prime ministerial residence.

Although some of her actions while in power were questionable, her dedication to her country and the people was unwavering. The night before she died she is reported to have said, 'I don't mind if my life goes in the service of the nation. If I die today every drop of my blood will invigorate the nation.' She's a woman who changed the world, who stood up for what she believed in and was prepared to defend it to the end.

WEATHER

❖

Signs, Clouds, Vocabulary and Famous Poems about the Weather

Weather Signs

METEOROLOGISTS USE DOPPLER radar, weather balloons, satellites and computers to give fairly accurate predictions of what the weather will be like in the near future. But even before we had computerized weather forecasts, we had ways to interpret and predict the weather. Generations ago, people passed down their knowledge about weather signs through rhymes and sayings they taught to their children. As it turns out, those rhyming proverbs based on the observations and wisdom of sailors, farmers and other outdoors people are grounded not only in experience but also in science. So if you're out camping, or hiking, or travelling on foot in nature, far away from technology, you can use some of that lore to determine a fairly reliable reading of the weather. Here are some of the most well-known rhymes about weather signs.

'Red sky at night, shepherd's delight. Red sky in morning, shepherd's warning'

The various colours of the sky are created by rays of sunlight that are split into colours of the spectrum as they bounce off water vapour and dust particles in our atmosphere. When the atmosphere is filled with lots of dust and moisture, the sunlight coming through it makes the sky appear reddish. This high concentration of particles usually indicates high pressure and stable air coming in from the west, and since weather systems usually move from west to east, that means you'll have good weather for the night. When the sun rises in the eastern sky looking red, that indicates a high water and dust content in the atmosphere, which basically means that a storm system may be moving in your direction. So if you notice a red sky in the morning, pack your umbrella.

'Ring around the moon, rain or snow soon'

You may have noticed some nights it looks like there's a ring around the moon. That halo, which can also form around the sun, is a layer of cirrus clouds composed of ice crystals that reflect the moon's light like prisms. These clouds are not rain- or snow-producing, but they sometimes show up as a warm front and low-pressure area approaches, which can mean inclement weather. The brighter the ring, the greater the chance of rain or snow.

'Clear moon, frost soon'

When the moon sits in a clear, cloudless sky, lore has it that frost is on its way. The weather science behind the saying explains that in a clear atmosphere, with no clouds to keep the heat on earth from radiating into space, a low-temperature night without wind encourages the formation of frost. When clouds cover the sky, they act as a blanket, keeping in the sun's heat absorbed by the earth during the day.

'A year of snow, a year of plenty'

This one seems a bit counter intuitive, but in fact a season of continuous snow is better for farmland and trees than a season of alternating warm and cold weather. When there's snow throughout the winter, that delays the blossoming of trees until the cold season is fully over. Otherwise, the alternate thawing and freezing that can come with less stable winter weather destroys fruit-bearing trees and winter grains.

'Rainbow in the morning gives you fair warning'

Rainbows always appear in the part of the sky opposite the sun. Most weather systems move from west to east, so a rainbow in the western sky, which would occur in the morning, signifies rain – it's giving you 'fair warning' about the rainstorm that may follow. (A rainbow in the eastern sky, conversely, tells you that the rain has already passed.)

EVERY GIRL'S TOOLBOX

❖

W ITH TOOLS YOU can make stuff, and that is a powerful feeling. You can help your grandfather finish that doll's house he's been tinkering with for years. You can make a swing for the garden, a bench for your den – or make the whole den.

Experiment with wood, nails, screws, hammers, screwdrivers and drills. After a while, you'll start to think in tools and materials, and you'll see how screws and nails hold wood together. Then you'll begin to come up with your own projects. Trial and error are the best teachers, and it doesn't take long to feel comfortable.

Visiting the DIY shop

Before we turn to the basic tools, a word on DIY shops. You might be intimidated by them, as many people are. Especially those antiquated-looking, small DIY shops, with their dusty shelves filled to the brim with unfamiliar, scary-looking objects, usually guarded by men who are burly and possibly gruff.

Fear not, we are here to tell you. Said shops mark the entrance to a world in which you can create and repair anything imaginable. And the shops' burly guardians? The truth is, they may look gruff, but usually they're very nice, and they love to problem-solve and to find the perfect nail or wire for you. Ask for help when you're matching bolts and nuts. Get their advice on what kind of drill bit will attach a wood plaque to the stone wall outside your house. They'll show you where to find DIY shop exotica, and they know fix-it secrets you'll never learn in books.

Besides, many of them have daughters, too, and you can bet they've taught their girls a thing or two about what to do with a hammer and a box of nails.

Creating your toolbox

Every girl needs her own toolbox. You can get a decent toolbox, with a latch and an organizing tray, for as little as ten pounds. Here are the basics to fill it with.

1 **Safety Glasses.** These are an absolute must when hammering, drilling or sawing.

2 **Claw Hammer.** The flat side of the hammer bangs nails into wood; the V-shaped claw side pulls them out.

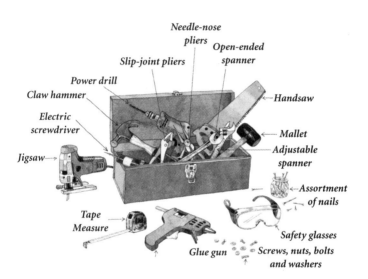

Needle-nose
pliers

Open-ended
spanner

Slip-joint pliers

Power drill

Claw hammer

Handsaw

Electric
screwdriver

Mallet

Adjustable
spanner

Jigsaw

Assortment
of nails

Tape
Measure

Safety glasses

Glue gun

Screws, nuts, bolts
and washers

EVERY GIRL'S TOOLBOX

To hammer, grip the handle solidly, near the bottom. Hold a nail with your thumb and forefinger, and tap it into the wood, gently, until it stands on its own. Then move your fingers away and hammer harder, from your forearm (that is, don't use your entire arm), and keep your wrist straight. Keep your eye on the nail, and trust your eye–hand coordination.

3 **Nails.** The measurements for nails derive from the custom of selling 100 nails for a certain number of pennies. Nails are thus described in pennyweights, except the resulting abbreviation is not p, but, oddly enough, d, in reference to an ancient Roman coin, the denarius.

Once upon a time you could walk into a store in Yorkshire and purchase 100 1½-inch nails for fourpence, and because of that, they are now labelled 4d nails after the old money. Much of the world, it must be said, uses the metric system for an easier and more reasonable way to measure nails.

4 **Screwdriver**. The screwdriver not only gets screws where they're going and takes them out; it can be used in a bazillion creative ways to do almost anything. Try a six-in-one screwdriver (which has six changeable heads). To get jobs done faster, we recommend a battery-operated screwdriver.

5 **Screws**. Screws and bolts live in those mysteriously thin cabinets in the back aisle of the hardware store, along with their friends, bolts, nuts and washers. Tighten a nut on a bolt to keep things ultra-secure. A washer – that's a flat circular object that slips on the bolt between the nut and the surface – protects the surface and helps tighten the nut.

Remembering the saying 'righty-tighty, lefty-loosy' will help you recall which direction to turn a screw.

6 **Spanner.** Spanners tighten and untighten the nuts that go at the end of bolts. They come in the open-end (fixed size) variety, and the adjustable. A small set of open-ended spanners, or one adjustable spanner, should start you off well.

7 **Pliers**. For gripping objects, like a stuck tap, get versatile slip-joint pliers. Also handy are needle-nose pliers to grab small objects, like wire. They often have a little wire cutter built in (peek at the intersection of the handles and you'll find it).

8 **Glue Gun**. When you can't use screws, bolts or nails, a glue gun saves the day, and is quite fun to operate. A small one should do, and don't forget plenty of glue sticks to melt in it.

9 **Tape Measure.** A 5-metre retractable tape measure that can lock in place is a good start.

10 **Saw**. A saw is not for the very young, of course, but it's a necessity for cutting wood to size and making shapes. A handsaw is a flat hand tool. A modern jigsaw is a power tool, activated by a trigger. All power tools are extremely dangerous if they are not used exactly as specified in their instructions, and you should always have adult supervision when operating them.

Hold long strips of wood on a sawhorse (a beam connected by four legs); cut small pieces of wood off the edge of a work table. Be careful, ask for help and, as always, use your safety glasses.

11 **Drill**. To drill, start with an awl or centre punch (hand tools that look like small spikes) to make an indentation in your surface so the drill bit won't slip.

A battery-operated power drill is very handy. It will come with a basic set of bits, or you can get a set if it doesn't. There's an art to matching up the right drill bit to the size of the hole you'll need for the screw. If you know the size of the bolt or screw, that helps. Otherwise, the best we can tell you is to peer closely at the sizes and when in doubt try the smaller bit first. Experience will make it all the more clear.

Once you have your own toolbox, you might begin to truly love the DIY shop. You'll stand for hours looking at the display of unique drill bits to make holes in metal, brick, plastic or stone; at the sander attachment that can remove paint or brush wood's rough edges clean; at the buffer that smooths it to perfection. You'll handle each one carefully, and after much deliberation with the burly bloke behind the counter about the pros and cons of each, take some home to try out on a project of your own imagination.

QUEENS OF THE ANCIENT WORLD I

Boudicca's Rebellion against Rome

BOUDICCA WAS A warrior queen, with a fierce way about her and brilliant red hair that flowed to her waist. As Queen of the Celtic tribe of the Iceni in the first century AD, Boudicca organized a revolt against the Romans, hoping to regain and protect her people's independence.

In the year 43 AD, Roman soldiers marched to the French edge of the European continent, crossed the Channel and began their invasion of Britain. The Emperor Claudius, whose reign had begun in 41 AD and would last until 54 AD, dreamed of conquering the mysterious British island. Rome was at the height of its power. Its huge army helped expand the boundaries of Rome in all directions. Britain was a special challenge. It sat beyond a choppy channel of water and was the furthest spot to the northwest that the Romans could imagine, with a cold, unfathomable and terrifyingly large sea beyond.

Britain was the home of Celtic tribes and Druids, with their mystical traditions and religious groves of trees. In Rome, the lives of women and girls were as controlled as the tightly wound hair braids and coils that were the fashion of the day. There, men dominated public life and women, especially those in wealthy and powerful families, lived more private lives. By contrast, Celtic women had many more rights. They could govern and make laws, marry more freely, own property and, alongside men, they could work and take part in their community's marketplace. Their hair, too,

Roman
Britain

Druids at
Mona Island

Iceni

Venta Cuistok

Catovellauni

Trinovantes

Camulodunum

Londinium

showed their freedom: the fashion was to grow it long and leave it down, ready to fly with the wind.

Boudicca was of the Iceni tribe, which inhabited the eastern part of Britain, and she had married Prasutagus, the tribe's king. As Roman legions invaded and took over the land of the Celts, Boudicca watched, unbelievingly. The Romans declared much of Britain to be the Roman province of Britannia. They founded the cities of Londinium – now called London – and Camulodunum (Colchester), which they made into their capital. There they built a massive Roman-style temple to the Emperor Claudius and a towering statue of a woman representing Victory.

Facing troops with greater weapons, the Iceni and nearby Celtic tribes followed the path of many local tribes. They feared that active resistance would mean death for many and slavery for the rest and so they submitted. When the Romans came to the Iceni kingdom, they decided that Prasutagus should continue to rule his people. The Iceni could remain semi-independent so long as they stayed loyal to Rome. The Romans often made arrangements like this, charging local rulers to keep the peace and to collect taxes for the Empire. Prasutagus' small kingdom lasted this way for nearly twenty years, until he died in the year 60 AD, leaving behind Boudicca and their two daughters.

Most of what we know about Boudicca's life comes to us from the Roman historian Tacitus, who in 109 AD wrote the

Annals, detailing Rome's first-century exploits. Tacitus reports that under Roman rule, Prasutagus and Boudicca remained prosperous. After Prasutagus' death, however, it was learned that he had been wheeling and dealing with the Romans and this included borrowing a great deal of money from the Roman governor. Prasutagus' will directed that half the kingdom be turned over to the Romans to pay his debt. The other half he gave to his two daughters, for them to rule as queens.

Prasutagus had hoped his deathbed directions would protect his family, but this didn't happen. The Roman governor Suetonius had already decided that when Prasutagus died, he would disarm the Iceni people, confiscate their arrows and spears and darts and annex their land fully into the Roman province of Britannia.

Roman soldiers soon arrived at Boudicca's palace to plunder Prasutagus' wealth and claim his entire kingdom as their own. They captured Boudicca and made a show of torturing her and her two daughters in front of the Iceni tribesmen and women. Their cousins, aunts and uncles were made into slaves.

Later that year, the Roman governor Suetonius decided to conquer Wales. As the soldiers of his fearsome legions marched westward, they left the cities of Camulodunum and Londinium largely undefended.

Boudicca sensed her chance. She claimed the mantle of leadership and stirred her people to reclaim their freedom and liberty. She reminded them of the horror and cruelty of Roman rule and rallied them to win back their lands.

Boudicca outlined her plan. Suetonius was in Wales, routing Druids on the Isle of Mona. Leading the way in her horse-drawn chariot, with 100,000 British fighters behind her, she would attack Camulodunum first. All around, miraculous omens pointed to Boudicca's success; ancient reports tell us that the city's Victory statue fell from its tall base to the ground below with no cause, as if Rome were already yielding.

Boudicca's troops stormed the city's gates. By day's end the city was in flames. A small group of Roman soldiers and leaders locked themselves inside the Temple of Claudius, holding out for two days until Boudicca burned the temple to the ground.

After hearing of Boudicca's victory at Camulodunum, the Roman governor Suetonius left Wales and headed straight back to London to protect it from Boudicca's rampaging soldiers. Seeing Boudicca's willingness to burn cities to the ground, he decided, however, to abandon London to her fires. Boudicca's soldiers left 25,000 people dead in London before advancing to Verulamium (St Albans), Britain's third-largest city, where they killed everyone who had cooperated with the Romans and then destroyed the city.

Boudicca's army began to falter. As Suetonius' men approached, they burned the crops in the fields, sending ripened corn and beans into smoke and leaving nothing to feed Boudicca's troops and keep them strong. Boudicca had successfully destroyed unarmed cities, but Suetonius and his professional legions were too strong for the relatively untrained British Celts, whose luck now turned. Boudicca fought one final battle, the place of which is unknown. Her troops had to start from the bottom of a tall hill and face off against the Romans, who were strategically encamped at the top. Roman arrows and pikes rained down on the Celts. Boudicca's fighters were overpowered and many were lost to battle.

The rebellion was over. As night fell, Boudicca abandoned the glorious bronze chariot that had served her well. She grabbed her two teenage daughters by the hand and together the three of them ran through the darkness, returning home to their palace along hidden paths and back roads. Once home, they knew they would be captured and brought to Rome to be displayed in chains to the jeering crowds at the Colosseum. Instead, Boudicca decided to end her own life by drinking a cup of poison and her princess daughters took the same route. It is said that when her closest relatives entered the palace, they found Boudicca wearing her legendary tunic of brilliant colours, covered with a deep auburn cloak, her flaming red hair still untamed.

DID YOU KNOW? ELEMENTS AND ATOMS

ELEMENTS ARE BASIC pieces of matter, composed of a single unique kind of atom. There is nothing that's not made of elements. We know of 111 natural elements and 7 that have been made only in the laboratory. Some elements – like silver, gold, tin, sulphur, copper and arsenic – were known in classical antiquity and native peoples of the Americas knew about platinum. Others were discovered during the Enlightenment and more recently.

* An atom is the basic building block of everything. A group of atoms is called a molecule and molecules form everything we know, live in and touch.

* Inside an atom are protons, neutrons, electrons, quarks and gluons, none of which are visible to our eyes, unfortunately.

* Protons are found in the atom's nucleus and carry a positive charge. Each element has a unique number of protons and the number of protons in an atom never changes. Hydrogen, H, always has 1 proton;

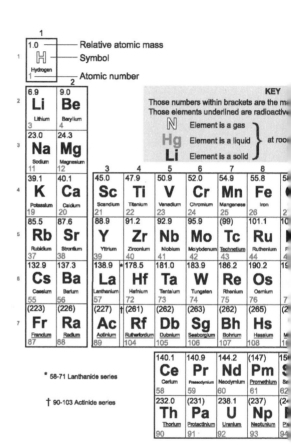

1								
1.0 — Relative atomic mass								
H — Symbol								
Hydrogen								
1 — Atomic number								

KEY

Those numbers within brackets are the m
Those elements underlined are radioactiv

Ⓝ Element is a gas
Hg Element is a liquid   } at roo
Li Element is a solid

2								
6.9 **Li** Lithium 3	9.0 **Be** Beryllium 4							
23.0 **Na** Sodium 11	24.3 **Mg** Magnesium 12	3	4	5	6	7	8	
39.1 **K** Potassium 19	40.1 **Ca** Calcium 20	45.0 **Sc** Scandium 21	47.9 **Ti** Titanium 22	50.9 **V** Vanadium 23	52.0 **Cr** Chromium 24	54.9 **Mn** Manganese 25	55.8 **Fe** Iron 2	5
85.5 **Rb** Rubidium 37	87.6 **Sr** Strontium 38	88.9 **Y** Yttrium 39	91.2 **Zr** Zirconium 40	92.9 **Nb** Niobium 41	95.9 **Mo** Molybdenum 42	(99) **Tc** Technetium 43	101.1 **Ru** Ruthenium 44	10
132.9 **Cs** Caesium 55	137.3 **Ba** Barium 56	138.9 **La** Lanthanium 57	*178.5 **Hf** Hafnium 72	181.0 **Ta** Tantalum 73	183.9 **W** Tungsten 74	186.2 **Re** Rhenium 75	190.2 **Os** Osmium 76	19
(223) **Fr** Francium 87	(226) **Ra** Radium 88	(227) **Ac** Actinium 89	†(261) **Rf** Rutherfordium 104	(262) **Db** Dubnium 105	(263) **Sg** Seaborgium 106	(262) **Bh** Bohrium 107	(265) **Hs** Hassium 1	(2

* 58-71 Lanthanide series

† 90-103 Actinide series

140.1 **Ce** Cerium 58	140.9 **Pr** Praseodymium 59	144.2 **Nd** Neodymium 60	(147) **Pm** Promethium 61	15 **S** Sa 62
232.0 **Th** Thorium 90	(231) **Pa** Protactinium 91	238.1 **U** Uranium 92	(237) **Np** Neptunium 93	(2 P 94

Periodic Table (partial)

					18
					4.0
					He
					Helium
					1

	13	14	15	16	17	18
mmon isotopes	10.8	12.0	14.0	16.0	19.0	20.2
	B	**C**	N	O	**F**	Ne
	Boron	Carbon	Nitrogen	Oxygen	Fluorine	Neon
	5	6	7	8	9	10
pressure	27.0	28.1	31.0	32.1	35.5	39.9
	Al	**Si**	**P**	**S**	Cl	Ar
	Aluminium	Silicon	Phosphorus	Sulphur	Chlorine	Argon
	13	14	15	16	17	18

11	12	13	14	15	16	17	18
3.5	65.4	69.7	72.6	74.9	79.0	79.9	83.8
Cu	**Zn**	**Ga**	**Ge**	**As**	**Se**	Br	Kr
Copper	Zinc	Gallium	Germanium	Arsenic	Selenium	Bromine	Krypton
9	30	31	32	33	34	35	36
07.9	112.4	114.8	118.7	121.8	127.6	126.9	131.3
Ag	**Cd**	**In**	**Sn**	**Sb**	**Te**	**I**	Xe
Silver	Cadmium	Indium	Tin	Antimony	Tellurium	Iodine	Xenon
7	48	49	50	51	52	53	54
97.0	200.6	204.4	207.2	209.0	(210)	(210)	(222)
Au	Hg	**Tl**	**Pb**	**Bi**	Po	At	Rn
Gold	Mercury	Thallium	Lead	Bismuth	Polonium	Astatine	Radon
9	80	81	82	83	84	85	86

7.3	158.9	162.5	164.9	167.3	168.9	173.0	175.0
Gd	**Tb**	**Dy**	**Ho**	**Er**	**Tm**	**Yb**	**Lu**
adolinium	Terbium	Dysprosium	Holmium	Erbium	Thulium	Ytterbium	Lutetium
	65	66	67	68	69	70	71
47)	(247)	(251)	(252)	(257)	(258)	(259)	(260)
Cm	**Bk**	**Cf**	**Es**	**Fm**	**Md**	**No**	**Lr**
Curium	Berkelium	Californium	Einsteinium	Fermium	Mendelevium	Nobelium	Lawrencium
	97	98	99	100	101	102	103

aluminium, Al, always has 13. The proton number distinguishes one element from the others, and accounts for each element's character and behaviour. The number of protons determines the order of elements on the Periodic Table. Os, or osmium, is not the random 76th element, it has 76 protons, and hence its place on the chart. Neutrons are in the nucleus, and carry a neutral charge.

* Both protons and neutrons break down into quarks, and quarks are held together by gluons.

* Electrons have a negative electrical charge and they orbit around the nucleus. The sharing of electrons between atoms creates bonds. In metals, the movement of electrons between atoms can generate electrical current.

* Four elements were discovered by female scientists.

Element	Abbreviation/ Atomic Number	Discovered By	Date
Polonium	Po/84	Marie Sklodowska Curie	1898
Radium	Ra/88	Marie Sklodowska Curie with her husband Pierre Curie	1898
Rhenium	Re/75	Ida Tacke-Noddack with her colleagues Walter Noddack and Otto Carl Berg	1925
Francium	Fr/87	Marguerite Catherine Perey	1939

PIRATES

❖

THERE HAVE BEEN women pirates throughout the ages, from Queen Artemisia to female Vikings to modern-day women pirates in the Philippines. Many of the stories about female pirates are just that: stories made up showcasing women pirates who are merely fictional. But there are several women pirates whose stories are verifiable, and who really did live and (in some cases) die a pirate's life on the high seas.

Charlotte Badger

Charlotte Badger was a convicted felon when she was sent to Australia from England. She was found guilty of the crime of breaking and entering when she was eighteen years old and sentenced to seven years' deportation. She sailed to Port Jackson, Sydney, aboard the convict ship *The Earl of Cornwallis* in 1801 and served five years of her sentence at a factory, during which time she also gave birth to a daughter.

With just two years of her sentence left, she was assigned to work as a servant to a settler in Hobart Town, Tasmania, along with fellow prisoner Catherine Hagerty. In April 1806, Charlotte, her daughter, Catherine, and several male convicts travelled to Hobart Town on a ship called *Venus*. When the *Venus* docked at Port Dalrymple in June, the convicts mutinied and Charlotte and her friend Catherine joined in with the male convicts to seize control of the ship. The pirate crew headed for New Zealand (even though nobody aboard really knew how to navigate the ship) and Charlotte, her child, Catherine, and two of the male convicts were dropped off at Rangihoua Bay in the Bay of Islands.

Charlotte and her compatriots built huts and lived on the shore of the island, but by 1807, Catherine Hagerty was dead and the two men had fled. The *Venus* had long since been overtaken by South Sea islanders, who captured the crew and then burned the ship. Charlotte and her child stayed on at Rangihoua Bay, living alongside the Maori islanders. Twice she was offered passage back to Port Jackson and twice she refused, saying that she preferred to die among the Maori.

What happened to Charlotte after 1807 isn't entirely clear. Some stories have her living with a Maori chieftain and bearing another child; in other stories the Maori turned on her, prompting her and her daughter to flee to Tonga; still other stories eventually place her in America, having stowed away on another ship. Whatever happened to her, she was quite possibly the first European woman to have lived in New Zealand and one of New Zealand's first women pirates.

Anne Bonny and Mary Read

Anne Bonny, born in Ireland around 1700, is by all accounts one of the best-known female pirates. She was disowned by her father when, as a young woman, she married a sailor named James Bonny; the newlyweds then left Ireland for the Bahamas. There, James worked as an informant, turning in pirates to the authorities for a tidy sum. While James confronted pirates, Anne befriended them: she became especially close to Jack Rackam, also known as 'Calico Jack'. Jack was a pirate who had sworn off pirating so as to receive amnesty from the Bahamian governor, who had promised

MARIE READ.

Mary Read

PIRATES

not to prosecute any pirate who gave up his pirating ways. In 1719, however, Anne and Jack ran off together and Jack promptly returned to pirating – this time with Anne by his side. She donned men's clothing in order to join the crew on his ship, the *Revenge*, and was so good at the work that she was accepted as a crewmate even by those men who discovered she was actually a woman.

When the *Revenge* took another ship during a raid and absorbed its crew, Anne discovered she was no longer the only woman on board: a woman by the name of Mary Read had also disguised herself as a man to be accepted as a pirate. Mary, born in London in the late 1600s, had spent nearly her whole life disguised as a man. Mary's mother had raised her as a boy almost from birth to keep the family out of poverty. (Mary's father died before she was born and her brother, who would have been the only legal heir, also died. Back then, only men could inherit wealth, so baby Mary became baby Mark.) As a young girl living as a boy, Mary worked as a messenger and eventually enlisted in the infantry, fighting in Flanders and serving with distinction. She fell in love with another soldier (to whom she revealed her true gender) and they soon married, leaving the army to run a tavern called The Three Horseshoes. Sadly, her husband died in 1717 and Mary once again had to disguise herself as a man to earn a living. She put on her dead husband's clothes, enlisted in the army and went to Holland.

Anne Bonny

PIRATES

She found no adventure there, so she boarded a ship for the West Indies. That was when her ship was captured by the *Revenge* and her life intersected with those of Calico Jack and his mistress, Anne Bonny.

Anne and Mary became close friends and once Anne knew the truth about Mary, she swore that she would never reveal Mary's true identity. But Calico Jack, jealous of Anne's attention, grew suspicious of their friendship and demanded an explanation. Soon the secret was out, but, luckily for Mary, Jack was relieved and not angered to discover she was a woman. He allowed her to continue on the crew, and just as Anne had been accepted by her crewmates despite being female, Mary was accepted too. Unfortunately for the crew of the *Revenge*, the Bahamian governor was not so accepting of pirates who flouted amnesty agreements by returning to pirating after promising not to, and he issued a proclamation naming Jack Rackam, Anne Bonny and Mary Read as 'Pirates and Enemies to the Crown of Great Britain'.

In 1720, the *Revenge* was attacked by a pirate-hunter eager to capture an enemy of the Crown. Calico Jack, along with nearly the entire crew, was drunk at the time and the men quickly retreated to hide below deck and wait out the attack. Only Anne and Mary stayed above, fighting for the ship. It is said that Anne shouted to the crew, 'If there's a man among ye, ye'll come out and fight like the men ye are thought to be!' Enraged by the crew's cowardice, Anne and

Mary shot at them, killing one man and wounding several others, including Calico Jack. Despite the women's efforts, the ship was captured.

The crew was taken to Jamaica and tried for piracy in November of 1720. All of them were hanged, save for Anne and Mary, who were granted stays of execution due to the fact that they were both pregnant. Mary was brave in the face of her punishment, telling the court, 'As to hanging, it is no great hardship. For were it not for that, every cowardly fellow would turn pirate and so unfit the sea, that men of courage must starve.' But as it turned out, Mary never had to face the gallows: she died in prison of a fever. As for Anne, after the piracy trial, the historical record is silent. Rumours say alternately that she was hanged a year later; that she was given a reprieve; that she reconciled with the father who disowned her, or with her first husband, whom she had left; that she gave up the pirate's life and became instead a nun. We may never know for sure what happened to her.

Ching Shih

Ching Shih – also known as Shi Xainggu, Cheng I Sao, Ching Yih Saou, or Zheng Yi Sao – ruled the South China Sea in the early nineteenth century, overseeing about 1,800 ships and 80,000 male and female pirates.

She became the commander of the infamous Red Flag Fleet of pirates after her husband Cheng Yi, the former commander from a long line of pirates, died in 1807; she went on to marry Chang Pao, formerly her husband's right-hand man. To say that Ching Shih ran a tight ship was an understatement: pirates who committed even innocuous offences were beheaded. Her attitude in battle was even more intense, with hundreds of ships and thousands of pirates used to engage even a small target.

Ching Shih was also a ruthless businesswoman. She handled all business matters herself, and pirates not only needed her approval to embark on a raid, they were also required to surrender the entire haul to her. She diversified her business plan by expanding beyond the raiding of commercial ships, working with shadowy businessmen in the Guangdong salt trade to extort the local salt merchants. Every ship passing through her waters had to buy protection from her and Ching Shih's fleet of mercenaries torched any vessel that refused to pay up.

The Red Flag Fleet under Ching Shih's rule could not be defeated – not by Chinese officials, not by the Portuguese navy, not even by the British. But in 1810, amnesty was offered to all pirates and Ching Shih took advantage of it, negotiating pardons for nearly all her troops. She retired with all her ill-gotten gains and ran a gambling house until her death in 1844.

Granuaile: Ireland's Pirate Queen, 1530–1603 by Anne Chambers

This book was made into a Broadway musical called *The Pirate Queen*. It tells the story of Grace O'Malley, also called Granuaile, a remarkable and notorious Irish pirate.

The Pirate Hunter: The True Story of Captain Kidd by Richard Zacks

A vivid account of the often brutal nature of pirate life and politics in the seventeenth century.

Under the Black Flag: The Romance and the Reality of Life Among the Pirates by David Cordingly

A look at the realities of the oft-romanticized pirate life through stories of real and fictitious pirates between 1650 and 1725.

The Pirates' Own Book: Authentic Narratives of the Most Celebrated Sea Robbers by Charles Ellms

Originally published in 1887, this book features pirates reporting in their own words.

Booty: Girl Pirates on the High Seas by Sara Lorimer

Stories of twelve women pirates from the ninth century to the 1930s.

Rachel Wall

Rachel Schmidt was born in Carlisle, Pennsylvania, in 1760. When she was sixteen, she met George Wall, a former privateer who served in the Revolutionary War; against the wishes of her mother, she married him. The two moved to Boston, where George worked as a fisherman and Rachel worked as a maid in Beacon Hill. George, whom Rachel's mother had considered more than slightly shady to begin with, fell in with a rough crowd and gambled away what money they had. Unable to pay the rent, and lured by the fun of his fast-living fisherman friends, he hit upon pirating as the answer to their financial woes and convinced Rachel to join in.

George and Rachel stole a ship at Essex and began working as pirates off the Isle of Shoals. They would trick passing ships by having the blue-eyed, brown-haired Rachel pose as a damsel in distress, standing at the ship's mast and screaming for help as ships floated by. Once the rescuing crew came aboard to help, George and his men would kill them, steal their booty and sink their ship. Rachel and George were successful as pirates, capturing a dozen boats, murdering two dozen sailors and stealing thousands of dollars in cash and valuables.

Their evil plan was cut short in 1782, when George, along with the rest of his crew, was drowned in a storm.

Rachel, who really did need rescuing in that situation, was saved, brought ashore and taken back to Boston, but it was hard to leave her pirating ways. She spent her days working as a maid, but by night she broke into the cabins of ships docked in Boston Harbor, stealing any goods she could get her hands on.

Her luck ran out in 1789, when she was accused of robbery. At her trial, she admitted to being a pirate but refused to confess to being a murderer or a thief. She was convicted and sentenced to death by hanging. She died on 8 October 1789, the first and possibly the only woman pirate in all of New England, and the last woman to be hanged in Massachusetts.

WOMEN WHO CHANGED THE WORLD

❖

The Suffrage Movement

THE RIGHT TO vote is something we tend to take for granted today, but it was hard won by women only a few generations ago. It is a part of history that is vital for every girl to know. You should never take for granted something so important.

The **1832 Reform Act** was instrumental in bringing into life the Women's Suffrage movement. It was passed with the intention of updating the voting system, which was agreed to be outdated and archaic, but it only gave suffrage (the right to vote) to men who owned property producing an annual income of over £10. This provoked debate about women's entitlement to suffrage, but it wasn't until forty years later that organized women's suffrage movements were first formed by women determined to get what they saw as their democratic rights.

SUFFRAGISTS V. SUFFRAGETTES

You may have heard both these names when people refer to the Women's Suffrage movement. They sound very similar, but they actually refer to two distinct groups of women who pursued two very different ways of achieving the same end.

Suffragists were on the whole a peaceful group whose aim was to achieve the vote for women through non-violent protest. In 1897 the National Union of Women's Suffrage Societies (NUWSS) was formed, with the intention of achieving the vote for women through education and democratic reform. Led by Millicent Fawcett, the group argued that women paid taxes, as men did, and ought to be afforded the same rights in choosing their government as men.

Suffragettes distinguished themselves from the Suffragists in that they were prepared to take violent and direct action to achieve their aims. They reasoned that the Suffragists were failing in their non-confrontational approach and that a more direct style was needed. So in 1903 Emmeline Pankhurst formed the Women's Social and Political Union (WSPU), a group that would take militant action. Its members, who included Pankhurst's daughters Christabel and Sylvia, chained themselves to railings, disrupted meetings, damaged property, and even firebombed and destroyed part of the

WOMEN WHO CHANGED THE WORLD:
THE SUFFRAGE MOVEMENT

house belonging to the prominent politician David Lloyd George, who was soon to become Prime Minister. And it was the Suffragettes who had their first martyr: Emily Davison who was killed when she threw herself under the King's horse at the Derby.

THE FIRST WORLD WAR

The activities of both groups were disrupted by the outbreak of the First World War as women set aside their protests in favour of patriotic activities in a time of war. But it was actually the war that allowed women to prove themselves. As the men went to fight, women were left to take over traditionally male roles in order to keep the economy running. Women worked as farm labourers, in munition factories, in aircraft manufacture. They also took on paid work just in order to survive financially and physically. Nursing was also a hugely important role, and women found themselves in the thick of war in a way they hadn't before.

VICTORY!

As the war drew to a close, the strength the women of Britain had demonstrated was rewarded as they were given the right to vote in 1918. It was a victory and a step towards equality, but it didn't go all the way. The right to vote was only extended to women over the age of thirty who were either householders or the wives of householders. It wasn't until 1928 that women were given the same rights as men, and women over the age of twenty-one were allowed to vote. In 1969 the voting age was lowered to eighteen, where it remains today.

IMPORTANT TERMS

The Cat and Mouse Act This was a law passed by Parliament in 1913 which allowed prisons to release inmates who were ill and also allowed for their re-imprisonment on their recovery. This Act was passed in response to the Suffragette hunger strikers who, once in prison, would refuse food as a continued political stand. Under the Act these women would be released once they became too weak to remain in prison, and in effect they were too weak to continue their struggle once they were free. If they committed another act of violence once they were out they could be re-arrested, where it was assumed that they would go back on hunger strike and the whole process would start again. It was an aggressive attempt by the government to try to control the Suffragette movement, but in reality it had very little effect.

WOMEN WHO CHANGED THE WORLD:
THE SUFFRAGE MOVEMENT

Enfranchise To give someone the vote, literally to liberate

NUWSS National Union of Women's Suffrage Societies, often called the Suffragists

Suffrage The civil right to vote

WSPU Women's Social and Political Union, often called the Suffragettes

KEY FIGURES

Emmeline Pankhurst is seen by many as the pre-eminent Suffragette. She was born Emmeline Gouldon in 1858 and in 1879 married Richard Pankhurst, himself a prominent supporter of women's rights. When Richard died suddenly in 1898, Emmeline threw herself into political activism on a greater scale. In 1903 she formed the Women's Social and Political Union (WSPU) and was instrumental in the militant action taken by the group. She was arrested several times and went on hunger strike while in prison. Undeterred, she continued her political activism. Once the First World War broke out she transferred her energies into making sure that women were allowed to take over the traditionally male jobs, organizing a mass rally of over 30,000 women in Hyde Park in 1914. Emmeline was still leading the WSPU in 1918 when women were enfranchised. She died at the age of sixty-eight, having achieved her goal.

Emily Davison was a passionate Suffragette. She was committed to the WSPU from its creation and voiced her call for women's suffrage through a series of direct actions which included breaking the windows of the House of Commons, arson attacks and, once in prison, hunger strikes. She strongly believed that it would take only one act of martyrdom to

WOMEN WHO CHANGED THE WORLD:
THE SUFFRAGE MOVEMENT

make the Establishment see sense and give women the vote. So in 1913 she made the ultimate sacrifice for her cause and threw herself under King George V's horse at the Derby. Little did she realize that this act would actually create more controversy, with men arguing that if this was the way women behaved they couldn't be trusted with the vote. She was buried with their slogan 'Deeds Not Words' on her headstone.

Millicent Fawcett founded the moderate National Union of Women's Suffrage Societies (NUWSS) in 1897 and was a leading Suffragist. Born Millicent Garrett in 1847, she saw the need for equality for women from a young age and, with her sisters Elizabeth and Emily, planned to study the male-dominated subjects of Politics, Medicine and Education (respectively). In the 1860s and early 1870s she was involved in a series of lectures for women that led to the foundation of Newnham College, Cambridge, the second college in the UK to admit women (the first being Girton College, Cambridge). As a Suffragist she distanced herself from the militant actions of the Suffragettes, which she saw as damaging to the cause and only alienating the Establishment. She died in 1929, just a year after women were given equal suffrage to men.

Josephine Butler was a passionate campaigner not only for women's rights but for the rights of all vulnerable people. She supported the fight for women's suffrage as she saw the role of women as one of caring and supporting the weak of the country, and she hoped that enabling women to vote would result in a more equal and socially responsible society as a whole. Born in 1828, she was somewhat older than many other leading women in the women's suffrage movement. She campaigned against the Contagious Diseases Act of the 1860s, which she saw as degrading to women; it was finally repealed in 1886. Josephine continued to support the Suffragists, and campaigned in particular against trafficking and the prostitution of women and children. She died in 1906 before women were enfranchised.

Rebecca West was a committed Suffragist. She began her writing life on the Suffragist magazine, the *Freewoman*, in 1911. She was born Cicily Fairfield but changed her name as she argued that her given name didn't inspire authority. She admired Emily Davison and Emmeline Pankhurst and wrote essays on each of them: 'The Sterner Sex' and 'The Reed of Steel'. She went on to become a well-respected novelist most famous perhaps for *The Return of the Soldier* and *The Fountain Overflows*. She was given a CBE in 1949 and became a Dame of the British Empire in 1959.

Women and voting around the world	
Country	Year of women's enfranchisement
USA	1869–1920 (individual states)
New Zealand	1893
Australia	1902
Finland	1906
Norway	1913
Denmark	1915
Canada	1917
Germany	1918
Poland	1918
Sweden	1921
Turkey	1926
South Africa	1930
India	1935
France	1945
Italy	1946

WOMEN WHO CHANGED THE WORLD:
THE SUFFRAGE MOVEMENT

Morocco	1963
Switzerland	1971
Liechtenstein	1984
Bahrain	2002
Oman	2003
Kuwait	2005

TONGUE TWISTERS

---◆---

HOW MUCH WOOD would a woodchuck chuck if a woodchuck could chuck wood?

Lots of children have spent break times rolling their tongues around this and other tongue twisters, but just how does a tongue twister work? In English sentences, similar sounds are usually separated so they are easier to say. Tongue twisters break this rule. They are filled to the brim with phonemes, which are sounds that differ only slightly from each other, like skunk and thunk and stunk, or mixed and biscuits. Tongue twisters are also filled with alliteration, which means that many of the words start with the same sound, as in *Sure the ship's shipshape, sir*. Because we don't usually say these sounds so quickly and close together, our brains get stumped and our tongues twisted.

Tongue twisters have long been used to teach proper and precise pronunciation to schoolchildren, since only with the clearest articulation might one stand a chance of saying these without a mumble. That makes them especially useful to twirl around your tongue to prepare for a play, a speech or any time you need to enunciate your syllables and separate your p's from your b's. People learning English for the first time have been known to practise tongue twisters to learn sounds.

Every language has tongue twisters. From the Wolof language of Senegal comes *Tuki fuki buki gudi. Tuki fuki buki becheck*, which means, *Travelling hyenas during the night, travelling hyenas during the day.* From Swedish comes *Barbros bror badade bara i Barsebäck*, which means *Barbra's brother only bathes in Barsebäck*, Barsebäck being a city in the south of Sweden.

Try saying these tongue twisters fives times fast, or ten:

She sold seashells on the seashore.

Peter Piper picked a peck of pickled peppers,
A peck of pickled peppers Peter Piper picked.
If Peter Piper picked a peck of pickled peppers,
How many pickled peppers did Peter Piper pick?
But if Peter Piper picked a peck of pickled peppers,
Were they pickled when he picked them from the vine?
Or was Peter Piper pickled when he picked the pickled
    peppers,
Peppers picked from the pickled pepper vine?

Red lorry, yellow lorry, red lorry, yellow lorry.

Betty Botter bought a bit of butter.
The butter Betty Botter bought was a bit bitter
And made her batter bitter.
But a bit of better butter
Makes batter better.
So Betty Botter bought a bit of better butter,
Making Betty Botter's bitter batter better.

PILOTS

------------- ◆ -------------

Amelia Earhart

A MELIA MARY EARHART, born in 1897, was a pilot who received the Distinguished Flying Cross – and worldwide fame – for being the first woman to fly solo across the Atlantic Ocean. During World War I, she trained as a nurse's aide through the Red Cross and worked in a hospital in Ontario, Canada, until after the war ended in 1918. Around that time she saw her first flying exhibition, and she was captivated. She stood her ground when one of the pilots flew low to buzz the crowd and later said of the experience, 'I did not understand it at the time, but I believe that little red airplane said something to me as it swished by.' The next year, she visited an airfield and was given a ride; a few hundred feet in the air and she was hooked. She began working odd jobs, including driving a truck and working at a telephone company, to earn money for flying lessons with female aviator Anita 'Neta' Snook. After six months of lessons, she bought her own plane, a used yellow biplane that she nicknamed 'The Canary' and in October 1922 she flew it to an altitude of 14,000 feet, setting a world record for women pilots. In May 1923, Earhart became the sixteenth woman to be issued a pilot's licence by the Fédération Aéronautique Internationale (FAI).

She not only broke aviation records, she also formed a women's flying organization (The Ninety-Nines) and wrote bestselling books. She was the first woman to fly across the Atlantic, the first woman to fly across the Atlantic alone and the first person, man or woman, to fly across the Atlantic

Amelia Earhart

PILOTS

alone twice. Earhart was also the first woman to fly an autogyro (a kind of flying craft) and the first person to cross the United States in an autogyro; the first person to fly solo across the Pacific between Honolulu and Oakland, California; the first person to fly solo non-stop from Mexico City to Newark, New Jersey; and the first woman to fly non-stop coast to coast across the United States. Her final accomplishment was becoming an enduring mystery: at the age of thirty-nine, in 1937, Amelia Earhart disappeared over the Pacific Ocean during an attempt at making a circumnavigational flight. The official search effort lasted nine days, but Amelia Earhart was never found.

In 1921, Bessie Coleman became the first woman to earn an international pilot's licence and the first black woman to

earn an aviator's licence. One of thirteen children, Coleman discovered aeroplanes after graduating from high school, but she couldn't find an aviation school that would teach a black woman to fly. She went to Paris, where she was able to train and earn her licence.

Jacqueline Cochran, who in 1953 became the first woman to break the sound barrier, holds more distance and speed records than any pilot, male or female. She was the first woman to take off from and land on an aircraft carrier; to reach Mach 2; to fly a fixed-wing jet aircraft across the Atlantic; to enter the Bendix Trans-continental Race; and to pilot a bomber across the north Atlantic. She was the first pilot to make a blind landing, the first woman in Ohio's Aviation Hall of Fame and the only woman ever to be president of the Fédération Aéronautique Internationale.

EXPLORERS

Alexandra David-Néel

ALEXANDRA DAVID-NÉEL, BORN Louise Eugénie Alexandrine Marie David (1868–1969), was the first European woman to travel to the forbidden city of Lhasa, Tibet, in 1924, when it was still closed to foreigners. She was a French explorer, spiritualist, Buddhist and writer, penning over thirty books on Eastern religion, philosophy and the experiences she had on her travels. By the time she was eighteen, she had already made solo trips to England, Spain and Switzerland, and when she was twenty-two, she went to India, returning to France only when she ran out of money. She married railway engineer Philippe Néel in 1904 and in 1911 she returned to India to study Buddhism at the royal monastery of Sikkim, where she met the Crown Prince Sidkeon Tulku. In 1912 she met the thirteenth Dalai Lama twice and was able to ask him questions about Buddhism. She deepened her study of spirituality when she spent two years living in a cave in Sikkim, near the Tibetan border. It was there that she met the young Sikkimese monk Aphur Yongden, who became her lifelong travelling companion, and whom she would later adopt. The two trespassed into Tibetan territory in 1916, meeting the Panchen Lama, but

Alexandra David-Néel

EXPLORERS

were evicted by British authorities. They left for Japan, travelled through China and in 1924 arrived in Lhasa, Tibet, disguised as pilgrims. They lived there for two months. In 1928, Alexandra separated from her husband and settled in Digne, France, where she spent the next ten years writing books about her adventures. She reconciled with her husband and travelled again with her adopted son in 1937, at the age of sixty-nine, going through the Soviet Union to China, India, and eventually Tachienlu, where she continued her study of Tibetan literature. It was an arduous journey that took nearly ten years to complete. She returned to Digne in 1946 to settle the estate of her husband, who had died in 1941, and again wrote books and gave lectures about what she had seen. Her last camping trip, at an Alpine lake in early winter, 2,240 metres above sea level, was at the age of eighty-two. She lived to be one hundred, dying just eighteen days before her one hundred and first birthday.

Freya Stark

Dame Freya Madeleine Stark (1893–1993) was a British travel writer, explorer and cartographer. She was one of the first Western women to travel the Arabian deserts and was fluent in Arabic and several other languages.

Freya Stark

Women Explorer Timeline

1704	Sarah Kemble Knight journeys on horseback, solo, from Boston to New York.
1876	Maria Spelternia is the first woman to cross Niagara Falls on a high wire.
1895	Annie Smith Peck becomes the first woman to climb the Matterhorn.
1901	Annie Taylor is the first person to go over Niagara Falls in a barrel.
1926	Gertrude Ederle is the first woman to swim the English Channel.
1947	Barbara Washburn becomes the first woman to climb Mount McKinley.
1963	Valentina Tereshkova becomes the first woman in space.
1975	Junko Tabei of Japan is the first woman to climb Mount Everest.
1976	Krystyna Choynowski-Liskiewicz of Poland is the first woman to sail around the world solo.
1984	Cosmonaut Svetlana Savitskaya becomes the first woman to walk in space.
1985	Tania Aebi, at nineteen, becomes the youngest person ever to sail alone around the world.

1985	Libby Riddles is the first woman to win the Iditarod Dog-Sled Race in Alaska.
1986	American Ann Bancroft becomes the first woman in the world to ski to the North Pole.
2001	Ann Bancroft and Norwegian Liv Arnesen are the first women to cross Antarctica on skis.
2005	Ellen MacArthur breaks the world record for sailing solo around the world.
2007	Eighteen-year-old Samantha Larson becomes the youngest person to climb the Seven Summits. (She and her father, Dr David Larson, are the first father-daughter team to complete the Seven Summits.)

RULES OF THE GAME: NETBALL

———————◆———————

THE FIRST GAMES of netball in the UK can be traced back to 1895 where it was played with a loose set of rules by ladies at Madame Ostenburg's College. Broadly based on the American game of basketball, it wasn't until Clara Baer, a US gymnastics teacher, formalized the rules that the more modern game of netball was born. Its popularity in Britain in the early twentieth century was huge and it soon spread like wildfire through the British Commonwealth. That's why netball now has a storied history in Australia, New Zealand, Jamaica, Barbados, Trinidad and Tobago, and India. Poly Netball Club, based in Chiswick, West London, holds claim to being the oldest netball club in the UK, harking back to their first recorded competitive game played in 1907. In 1995, netball was recognized as an Olympic sport, but it has not yet been added to the roster of competition.

Played with a ball slightly smaller than a football, netball is primarily played by girls. The uniform is usually gym skirts with bibs to show what position each girl is playing in.

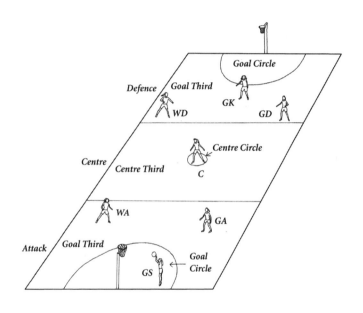

Goal Circle

Defence   *Goal Third*

GK

WD   *GD*

Centre Circle

Centre   *Centre Third*

C

WA   *GA*

Attack   *Goal Third*

Goal Circle

GS

SOME THINGS TO KNOW

1 Netball is a game of passing; there is no dribbling. You don't bounce the ball and run the full length of the court. The netball court is divided into three zones. Players are limited to specific thirds of the court and they pass the ball quickly, from one zone to another. A player with the ball must pass to the next player within three seconds. She can pass the ball within a zone or into the next zone, but can neither skip a zone, nor throw the ball way down the court.

2 A netball team has seven active positions. Each player has a particular position, one opposing player she defends against and a specific part of the court she plays in.

3 A player with the ball cannot run. Instead, netball players perfect the pivot and move their bodies while keeping one foot planted on the court. Fouls committed against these rules, breaking the three-second rule, or the ball going offside result in a free pass by the opposing team.

4 The basket is suspended on a three-metre-high pole. There is no backboard. To make a goal, one stands within the goal circle, aims for the front or back of the rim, and

shoots high, with some backspin. Oh, and no jumpshots, as at least one foot must stay on the floor. Each goal is worth one point, though a goal shot from outside the goal circle yields two points.

Netball Positions			
Abbreviation	**Position**	**Defends against the:**	**Playing Area**
GS	Goal Shooter	GK: Goal Keeper	A, goal circle
GA	Goal Attack	GD: Goal Defence	A and C, goal circle
WA	Wing Attack	WD: Wing Defence	A and C, not goal circle
C	Centre	C: Centre	All thirds, not goal circles
WD	Wing Defence	WA: Wing Attack	C and D, not goal circle
GD	Goal Defence	GA: Goal Attack	C and D, goal circle
GK	Goal Keeper	GS: Goal Shooter	D, goal circle

5 Defence players can intercept passes any way they like, but they cannot charge, intimidate or move closer than ninety centimetres towards the player with the ball. Moving in too close is called obstruction and results in a penalty pass.

6 A game has four fifteen-minute quarters, with three minutes between the first two and the last two, and a luxurious five-minute break at halftime.

7 Netball is a no-contact sport, which means players cannot push, trip, knock, bump, elbow, hold or charge each other. Although a player should attempt to intercept the ball while it is being passed, grabbing the ball while another player holds it is considered a foul. Breaking the personal contact rule results in a penalty pass for the opposing team and a penalty shot should any of this – or any untoward attempt to move the goalpost – happen within the goal circle.

ALL ABOUT ZERO

ZERO IS A mysterious number. It is nothing, absence, emptiness. But it is also something: a placeholder, a marker, a separator. Zero has the distinction of being both a thing and an idea, a quality and a quantity. Here are some amazing facts about zero.

Words for zero around the world

In French, it is *zéro*. In Italian, the word zero began as *zefiro*, which resembles the Latin and Greek words *zephyrus* and *zephyrum*, all meaning 'west wind'. In Arabic, zero is *sifr*, which evolved from the words *cifra*, and *safira* ('it was empty'); our word *cipher* is a descendant of these terms as well. In German, zero is *null*. And in Sanskrit zero is *śūnya* ('void' or 'empty'). English has many words for zero: aught, blank, cipher, dud, dummy, goose egg, nada, nadir, naught, nil, nix, nothing, null, void and zilch, to name a few.

Zero in history

* The ancient Chinese, Egyptians and Greeks did not have a symbol for zero.

* No one knows who invented zero, but some of the earliest examples of zero being used as a placeholder (distinguishing, say, 29 from 209) were found in Babylonian cuneiform tablets dating from around 300 or 400 BC.

* Interestingly, however, the Babylonians had used a mathematical system without zero for over a thousand years before they hit upon the idea of zero.

* The idea of zero as a number (rather than just a place-holder) was developed in India around the fifth century.

* The Italian mathematician Leonardo Fibonacci, who grew up in North Africa and studied Arabic and Hindu mathematics, introduced the concept of zero (which he called *zephyrum*) to Europe in the twelfth century. (For more on Fibonacci, see page 164.)

Fascinating Facts

* On a roulette wheel, which features numbers 1 to 36 in alternating red and black, the number zero is green. (American roulette wheels even have a second green spot – marked double-zero, 00.)

* In tennis, a score of zero is called 'love' – from the French *l'oeuf*, or egg, because of the way zero resembles an egg-shape. In other sports, too, you may have noticed announcers referring to a score of zero as 'a big goose egg'.

* A tarot card deck has 22 'trump' cards decorated with illustrations of people and symbolic scenes. Card number zero is 'The Fool'. The Fool is usually depicted as a ragged but happy vagabond with tattered clothes and a stick on his back carrying all his worldly possessions. And rather than being 'foolish' in the way we think of the world, he is meant to symbolize child-like wonder and curiosity, and the endless possibility of experience.

* On telephones, the zero comes after the number 9 instead of before the number 1. When it is pressed by itself, and not within a sequence of other numbers, it summons the operator.

＊ Anton Bruckner and Alfred Schnittke are the only composers of classical music to write a symphony titled Symphony No. 0. Bruckner also wrote a symphony called Symphony No. 00.

Zero, the spooky coincidence, and Tecumseh's Curse

Tecumseh (whose name means 'he who walks across the sky') was a Shawnee leader who rallied Native American tribes to defend their land in the early 1800s. During the Battle of Tippecanoe in 1811, he was killed by troops commanded by military leader William Henry Harrison. Harrison went on to become the ninth president of the United States – but he died of pneumonia only 31 days into his term. It is the briefest term in history and he was the first president to die while in office. A legend has grown up around this series of events, called 'the zero factor' or 'Tecumseh's Curse'. The story has it that Tecumseh's brother placed a curse on Harrison, and in fact on every president elected in a year ending in the number zero: they would all be doomed to die in office. If we go along with the premise that a curse was indeed made, it seems to have had a remarkably long run in terms of accuracy. Harrison was elected in 1840 and died after just 31 days. Presidents Lincoln (1860), Garfield (1880), and McKinley

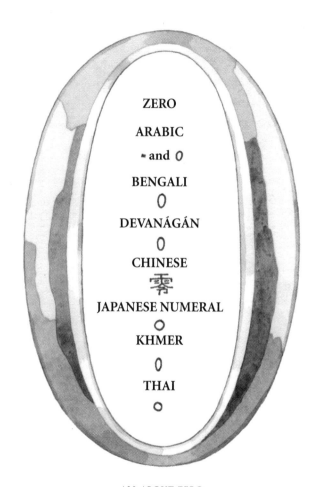

ZERO

ARABIC

and

BENGALI

DEVANÁGÁN

CHINESE

零

JAPANESE NUMERAL

KHMER

THAI

(elected to a second term in 1900) were all assassinated. Harding (1920) died of a stroke. Roosevelt (elected to a third term in 1940) died of a cerebral haemorrhage. Kennedy (1960) was assassinated. But Ronald Reagan, who was elected in 1980, survived an assassination attempt, and George W. Bush, who was first elected in 2000, seems to have escaped the curse unscathed. We will have to wait until the elections of 2020 to see if the curse has finally been lifted.

EMILY DICKINSON

———— ◆ ————

EMILY DICKINSON LIVED from 1830 to 1886 in Amherst, Massachusetts. She was a private person (her reclusive nature was the focus of the Tony Award winning play about her, *The Belle of Amherst*), but she left the world an incredible legacy of poetry exploring life, love, philosophy, nature and the human spirit. Her poetry was sharply dissimilar to the poetry written around that time, with her creative use of punctuation and the way her work veered between poetry and prose. She wrote to express herself and to make sense of the world around her – one particularly intense year saw her writing 300 poems! – and was encouraged in her literary efforts by a mentor at the *Atlantic Monthly* who pronounced her a 'wholly new and poetic genius'. Still, only seven of her poems were published during her lifetime, and anonymously at that, so she never lived to see the critical response her poetry generated. Now she is held alongside Walt Whitman as one of the two great founders of the American poetic tradition.

Here are seven of her most famous poems.

Hope is the thing with feathers
That perches in the soul
And sings the tune without the words
And never stops at all

And sweetest in the gale is heard;
And sore must be the storm
That could abash the little bird
That kept so many warm

I've heard it in the chillest land
And on the strangest sea
Yet, never, in extremity,
It asked a crumb of me.

EMILY DICKINSON

I'm nobody! Who are you?
Are you nobody too?
Then there's a pair of us don't tell!
They'd banish us you know.
How dreary to be somebody!
How public like a frog
To tell your name the livelong day
To an admiring bog!

EMILY DICKINSON

My life closed twice before its close
It yet remains to see
If Immortality unveil
A third event to me.

So huge, so hopeless to conceive,
As these that twice befell.
Parting is all we know of heaven,
And all we need of hell.

EMILY DICKINSON

This is my letter to the World
That never wrote to Me
The simple News that Nature told
With tender Majesty
Her Message is committed
To Hands I cannot see
For love of Her
Sweet countrymen
Judge tenderly of Me.

EMILY DICKINSON

There is no frigate like a book
To take us lands away,
Nor any coursers like a page
Of prancing poetry

This traverse may the poorest take
Without oppress of toll
How frugal is the chariot
That bears a human soul!

EMILY DICKINSON

I dwell in Possibility
A fairer House than Prose
More numerous of Windows
Superior for Doors
Of Chambers as the Cedar
Impregnable of Eye
And for an Everlasting Roof
The Gambrels of the Sky
Of Visitors the fairest
For Occupation This
The spreading wide my narrow
Hands To gather Paradise

EMILY DICKINSON

Because I could not stop for Death
He kindly stopped for me
The Carriage held but just Ourselves
And Immortality.

We slowly drove, He knew no haste
And I had put away
My labour and my leisure too,
For His Civility

We passed the School, where Children strove
At Recess, in the Ring
We passed the Fields of Gazing Grain
We passed the Setting Sun

Or rather He passed Us
The Dews drew quivering and chill
For only Gossamer, my Gown
My Tippet only Tulle

We paused before a House that seemed
A Swelling of the Ground
The Roof was scarcely visible
The Cornice in the Ground

Since then 'tis Centuries and yet
Feels shorter than the Day
I first surmised the Horses Heads
Were toward Eternity—

EMILY DICKINSON

QUEENS OF THE ANCIENT WORLD II

Wise Artemisia

I T IS A mystery what Queen Artemisia, who lived during the fifth century BC, looked like; no depictions of her survive. But the tales we know of her from the world's first historian, Herodotus, portray Artemisia as an intelligent and clever queen who bravely spoke her mind, even when no one else agreed with her. We also know she was a skilful and courageous sailor, who protected the Persian fleet during the ancient Greco-Persian Wars.

In the fifth century BC, Artemisia ruled Halicarnassus (today called Bodrum), a city nestled along a cove on the south-eastern coast of Turkey's Aegean Sea. Artemisia's father and her husband had ruled the city before her. When her husband died, she became queen, as their son was too young to rule.

At this time, in 480 BC, the Persian Empire was at its zenith. Xerxes (pronounced *Zerk-siz*), the fourth of the great Persian kings, was in power. He had already conquered much of Asia and turned his sights towards the Greek city-states and isles.

Xerxes narrowly won the battle of Thermopylae, capturing the pass to the Greek mainland, and then burned down its capital, Athens. He next headed south to take the island of Salamis, moving his battle to sea and relying heavily on the boats in his navy. He asked his allies around the Aegean Sea to send reinforcements. Loyal to Persia, Artemisia loaned five ships to Xerxes' war effort, large triremes, each with a grand sail, and powered by men from Halicarnassus rowing with long oars out the sides. She herself took command.

Yet Artemisia was different from many ancient queens (and kings), whom we are told wanted only to wage war. When Xerxes asked his general Mardonius to gather the commanders for counsel before storming Salamis, they all encouraged him to go ahead with the sea battle and assured him of victory. Except Artemisia. She warned Xerxes that the Greek ships were stronger than their own. She reminded him that he already held Greece's mainland with Athens and had lost many troops at Thermopylae. She contradicted all the other commanders in advising him to quit while he was ahead.

Xerxes admired Artemisia, but he decided, fatefully, to go with the opinion of the majority. The battle went wrong – terribly wrong – as Artemisia had predicted. Battle's end found the Persians watching from shore as their ships burned. Still, Artemisia kept her word to Xerxes and commanded her ship. She came under pursuit by an

Athenian ship and faced a terrible decision either to be captured or to run into the Persian ships that were ahead of her.

Artemisia made the decision to save her crew, ramming one of her allies' ships and sinking it in the effort to escape from the Greek ship. Some have said that she had a long-standing grudge against its commander, King Damasithymos of Calyndia. The commander of the Greek vessel chasing her turned away, assuming perhaps she was a sister Greek ship, or even a deserter from the Persian navy. The Persians lost the battle at Salamis, all the men on the Calyndian ship died, but Artemisia and her crew escaped unharmed.

After that battle, Herodotus tells us, King Xerxes again sought advice from his commanders. And again all the commanders wanted to stay and fight for the Grecian islands, except Artemisia. Disagreeing with the group once more, the level-headed queen counselled Xerxes to consider another option: leave 300,000 soldiers behind to hold the mainland and return to Persia himself with the rest of his navy.

Artemisia reminded Xerxes for a second time that he had already torched Athens and taken the Greek city-states. It was enough. The king took Artemisia's wisdom more seriously this time, knowing she had been right before. He listened to the wise woman over the majority, choosing to leave a contingent of troops in Greece and turn towards home instead of fighting.

MAVSOLÆVM.

MAVSOLI A BVSTO CALIDOS HAVRIRE MA
DEPOSCENS CONIVNX CINERES, PIETATIS ADVI

LIO) POSVIT TVMVLVM, SPIRANTIA CVIVS
GES, SVMMI CÆLARVNT MARMORE SIGNA

QUEENS OF THE ANCIENT WORLD II: WISE ARTEMISIA

And after that? Herodotus makes a brief mention of Artemisia ushering Xerxes' sons from Greece to safety in the city of Ephesus, on the Turkish mainland. After that, we have no further information about Artemisia's life. Herodotus concerns himself with describing the next battle, and the next, and because Artemisia declines to fight, she disappears from his pages.

A small vase provides our last evidence of Artemisia: a white jar made of calcite that is now at the British Museum. Xerxes gave the jar to Artemisia, a gift for her loyalty and service, and he inscribed it with his royal signature. Artemisia must have bequeathed the jar to her son, and from there, it stayed a family treasure for generations. One hundred years later, another member of her royal line, also named Artemisia, built a burial monument to her husband – the Mausoleum of Halicarnassus, one of the Seven Wonders of the Ancient World. There, in the 1850s, the British archaeologist Charles Newton excavated Xerxes' gift to the first Artemisia and uncovered the final trace of the wise queen.

CLOUDS

THE TERMS FOR categorizing clouds were developed by Luke Howard, a London pharmacist and amateur meteorologist, in the early 1800s. Before this, clouds were merely described by how they appeared to the viewer: grey, puffy, fleece, towers and castles, white, dark. Shortly before Howard came up with his cloud names, a few other weather scientists started devising cloud terminology of their own. But it was ultimately Howard's names, based on Latin descriptive terms, that stuck.

Howard named three main types of clouds: cumulus, stratus and cirrus. Clouds that carried precipitation he called 'nimbus', the Latin word for rain.

Cumulus

Cumulus is Latin for 'heap' or 'pile', so it makes sense that cumulus clouds are recognizable by their puffy cotton-ball-like appearance. These types of clouds are formed when warm and moist air is pushed upwards, and their size depends on the force of that upward movement and the amount of water in the air. Cumulus clouds that are full of rain are called cumulonimbus.

Stratus

Stratus clouds are named for their layered, flat, stretched-out appearance, as 'stratus' is the Latin word for layer. These clouds can look like a huge blanket across the sky.

Cirrus

Cirrus clouds are named for their wispy, feathery look. 'Cirrus' means 'curl of hair' and looking at cirrus clouds you can see why Luke Howard thought to describe them that way. These clouds form only at high altitudes and are so thin that sunlight can pass all the way through them.

CLOUDS

Nimbus

Nimbus clouds, the rain clouds, can have any structure or none at all. If you've seen the sky on a rainy day and it looks like one big giant grey cloud, you'll know what we mean.

DID YOU KNOW? HAIKU

* Haiku is a Japanese form of poetry. In English, a haiku consists of three lines: the first line has 5 syllables, the second has 7 and the last has 5.

* When writing haiku, it is considered traditional to include a kigo, or 'season word' to place the poem in a seasonal context and connect it to the temporal, cyclical aspect of nature; however, a kigo is not absolutely required.

* One of the hallmarks of haiku is its sense of immediacy: haiku is all about the present moment, and the essence of that moment, whether ordinary or extraordinary.

* One of the greatest female Japanese haiku poets was Chiyo-ni, who lived from 1703 to 1775. The daughter of a picture framer, she became the disciple of the famous poet Basho when she was twelve. By seventeen

her poetry was well known throughout Japan. Her most famous poem is 'Morning Glory'.

A morning glory
Twined round the bucket:
I will ask my neighbour for water.

CAT'S CRADLE

❖

CAT'S CRADLE IS a fun game played with two people and a length of string. It's been around for centuries and, perhaps because it is so simple, it remains popular today. There are lots of shapes you can make; here are a few to begin with.

You will need

* a long piece of string, perhaps a metre in length, tied at the ends so it forms a circle

* a friend to play with

First put your hands inside the circle of string, with your thumbs sticking out of the circle.

Then loop the string around your hands so it crosses your palms.

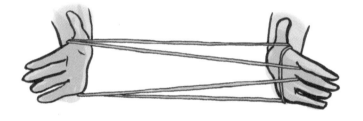

With your middle finger, pull the loop that crosses the opposite palm.

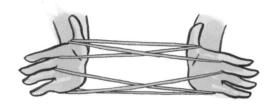

Repeat with the other hand.

This is the 'Cat's Cradle'. But this is just the beginning. Keep going!

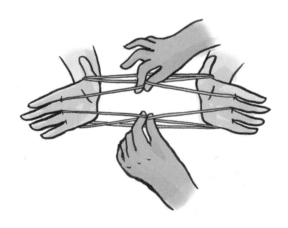

Your friend should take hold of the crosses – one on each side of the cat's cradle – with her forefingers.

Then she pulls them out and pushes them under and up through the middle of the cradle. You should then let go of the string so it ends up on your friend's hands.

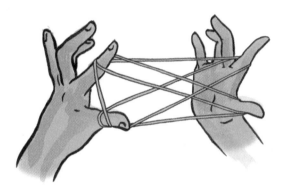

Now you take hold of the crosses from the top and pull them out, under and up through the middle, taking the string back from your friend.

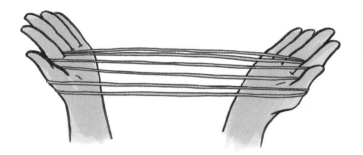

Now you have the 'Candles'. Here it gets a little complicated. Your friend needs to take one of the long middle strings with her little finger and pull it across to the other side. Then she does the same with the other long piece of string.

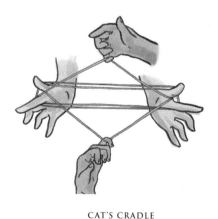

CAT'S CRADLE

Then she turns her hands downwards, into the triangles this has formed, and goes under, remembering to keep hold with her little fingers.

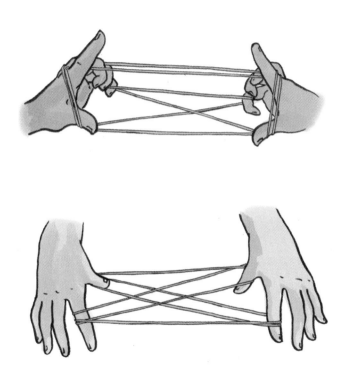

This is the 'Manger'. Now you take over, grabbing the crosses from the side and pulling them out, over and this time down into the middle, so you end up with the string formation on your hands with your hands pointing downwards.

You can keep going and get ever more complicated. Have fun practising!

WOMEN WHO CHANGED
THE WORLD

---◆---

Mary Wollstonecraft (1759–97)

MARY WOLLSTONECRAFT LIVED in volatile and uncertain times. The monarch, King George III, had lost his mind, causing what was known as the Regency Crisis. Over the Channel in France, revolution was stirring. The Bastille was stormed, the palace at Versailles was attacked and the French king, Louis XVI, and his queen, Marie Antoinette, along with most of their court, were executed by the people.

The sense of change and revolution led many people to question the ways in which they lived and opened up a vibrant debate among political thinkers and writers. Mary Wollstonecraft was key to this scene, and her writings would lead to a dramatic change in the lives of women and the way they were viewed in society.

Wollstonecraft is mostly known for her turbulent and unconventional life. She was a passionate woman who loved two men deeply in her lifetime. The first was George Imray, an American, with whom she moved to France in the 1790s. They had a daughter together but their affair was blighted by Imray's infidelities and they parted company. Wollstonecraft, much affected by this split, attempted suicide twice but was

unsuccessful. She then met William Godwin, an English writer, whom she married. Their daughter Mary would later marry the poet Shelley and would become well known in her own right for writing the gothic novel *Frankenstein*.

However, it was Wollstonecraft's writing that changed the world. She worked as a governess, and her experiences led her to question the education of women in society. The French philosopher Rousseau thought that women's education should be cultivated only for the entertainment of men, and his views were echoed by men across the country. But Wollstonecraft saw this as an attempt by men to control women and to keep them, through lack of education, as inferiors to men. Women, she argued in her seminal work, *A Vindication of the Rights of Woman*, were just as capable and intelligent as men, and if only they were given an equal education society would benefit. This seems sensible to us nowadays, but at the time it was a radical suggestion and one that many people, women and men, disagreed with strongly.

In Wollstonecraft's view, the education of women would lead to a more equal relationship between men and women and would also better equip women to act as companions to men, standing at their side intellectually rather than beneath them. She attacked the fashionable notion of 'sensibility', which meant an excess of emotion and a lack of rational thought, or 'sense'. You might recognize this debate from the title of one of Jane Austen's most popular novels: *Sense and Sensibility*.

Wollstonecraft's writings started an argument about the role of women in society, and many see her as a forerunner of the suffrage movement that would result in women winning the vote and gaining political equality. She wasn't particularly popular during her lifetime or in the years after she died – people looked down on what they saw as her dissolute life – but *A Vindication of the Rights of Woman* has become one of the most important books written at the time.

WOMEN SPIES

---◆---

Hedy Lamarr

HEDWIG EVA MARIA KIESLER is best known as Hedy Lamarr, film star of the 1930s and '40s. But she was also an inventor who patented an idea that was to become the key to modern wireless communication. During World War II, Hedy, along with George Antheil, invented a way to make military communications secure through frequency-hopping, an early form of a technology called spread spectrum. Hedy's status as a beautiful and successful actress provided her with the perfect cover: she was able to visit a variety of venues on tour and interact with many people, none of whom suspected that the stunning starlet might be listening closely and thinking of ways to help the US cause.

Princess Noor-un-nisa Inayat Khan

Princess Noor-un-nisa Inayat Khan was an author and a heroine of the French Resistance. The Princess trained as a wireless operator in Britain and was sent into occupied France as a spy with the code name 'Madeleine'. She became

Hedy Lamarr

Two famous and controversial World War I women spies, both of whom were executed, were Mata Hari (born Margaretha Geertruida Zelle McLeod) and Edith Cavell. Mata Hari was a dancer who used her vocation as a cover for her spy work for the Germans. She was shot by the French as a spy in 1917. Edith Cavell was a British nurse who worked in Belgium during the war. She secretly helped British, French and Belgian soldiers escape from behind the German lines, and she hid refugees in the nursing school she ran. By 1915 she had helped more than 200 soldiers, but the Germans grew suspicious and arrested her. She was executed by firing squad.

the sole communications link between her unit of the French Resistance and home base before she was captured by the Gestapo and executed.

The Girl Guides

During the First World War, the Girl Guides were used as couriers for secret messages by MI5, Britain's counterintelligence agency. Messengers were needed to work in the War

WOMEN SPIES

WOMEN SPIES

Office at the time, and at first Boy Scouts were used. But they proved to be difficult to manage, so Girl Guides were asked to serve instead. The girls, most of whom were between fourteen and eighteen years old, ran messages and patrolled on the roof; for their efforts they were paid ten shillings a week, plus food. Like all employees of MI5, they took a pledge of secrecy. But unlike many employees of MI5, they were among the least likely spies to arouse suspicion.

Virginia Hall

Virginia Hall, originally from the USA, spied for the French during World War II. She was chased by the Nazis over the Pyrenees into Spain and eluded them, even though she had a wooden leg. After escaping, she trained as a radio operator and transferred to the OSS, America's secret spy agency. In 1943 she returned to France as an undercover agent, gathering intelligence, helping to coordinate air drops in support of D-Day, and working with the French underground to disrupt German communications. After the war, Virginia was awarded America's Distinguished Service Cross, the only American civilian woman to receive such an honour. She continued to work for the OSS, and later the CIA, until her retirement in 1966.

Violette Szabo

Violette Bushell Szabo was recruited and trained by the British Special Operations Executive after her husband, a member of the French Foreign Legion, was killed in North Africa. She was sent to France, where she was captured during a shoot-out. She refused to give up her information and was sent to the Ravensbruck concentration camp, where she was eventually killed. She was awarded the George Cross and the Croix de Guerre posthumously in 1946.

Josephine Baker

Josephine Baker was another World War II-era entertainer whose celebrity status helped distract from her mission as a spy. Josephine was a dancer and singer from the US. She moved to Paris when she was nineteen and became an international star. When World War II began, she started working as an undercover operative for the French Resistance, transporting orders and maps from the Resistance into countries occupied by Germany. Her fame and renown made it easy for her to pass unsuspected, as foreign officials were thrilled to meet such a famous performer, but she wrote the secret information in disappearing ink on her sheet music just in case.

Josephine Baker

Amy Elizabeth Thorpe

Amy Elizabeth Thorpe, also known as Betty Pack and 'Code Name Cynthia', was an American spy first recruited by the British secret service and later by the American OSS. She is probably best remembered for her procurement of French naval codes, necessary for the Allies' invasion of North Africa, which she accomplished by tricking a man connected to the Vichy French Embassy into giving them to her. Not only did she steal French naval code books from the safe in his locked room, she also stole his heart: after the war they were married, and they spent the rest of their lives together.

Margery Urquhart

Margery Urquhart was the first woman ever to work for Special Branch. Born to Scottish parents in Chile, she was recruited into espionage work in 1935 and then became a spy for Britain during the Second World War. She was integral to the counter-espionage activity against the Germans. When the war ended she continued her work, and during her long career she worked on cases of terrorism in the UK. She later became a police officer with Surrey police and received the OBE in 1977 for service to her country.

LAYERS OF THE EARTH

———— ◆ ————

THE EARTH IS made up of several distinct layers, from the relatively cool, thin outer crust, to the warm thick mantle, to the fiery hot and deep core.

Crust

The Earth's outer shell consists of two parts: the oceanic crust and the continental crust.

The continental crust (the ground, to you and me) is the second smallest area of the Earth and can be anywhere from 20 to 45 miles thick. This layer is mostly made up of granite, though it also contains silicon, aluminium, calcium, sodium and potassium.

The oceanic crust (or what we might think of as the bottom of the sea) is the smallest part of the Earth. It is between 3 and 6 miles thick, and most of the ocean floor is composed mostly of basalt (a type of rock) generated from volcanic activity. (Hawaii and Iceland are two island clusters that came into existence from accumulated basalt.) This thin, oceanic layer is also where new crust is formed. The crust is divided into continental plates, which drift a few centimetres each year across the Earth's mantle.

Mantle

The Earth's mantle, at 1,800 miles thick, is the largest inner layer. Like the crust, it also has two main sections: the upper mantle and the lower mantle. Together, the crust and the upper mantle are referred to as the lithosphere (from the Greek words *lithos* or rocky, and *sphaira* ball).

The upper mantle is rigid rock, including basaltic magma (molten rock) and garnet peridotite. Volcano excavations have shown that the mantle is made of crystalline forms of olivine (a mineral, one of the most common ones on Earth) and pyroxene (a kind of rock-forming silicate mineral, which is a mineral containing silicon and oxygen). But it's not entirely solid: the part of the upper mantle called the asthenosphere (from the Greek *a* meaning without, plus *sthenos* strength; so, 'without strength'), which is about 125 miles below the surface, is a weak, soft zone that seems to be molten and flexible rather than rigid like the rest of the upper mantle.

The lower mantle is made up of many chemicals, including silicon, magnesium, oxygen, iron, calcium and aluminium. It is dense, very hot – temperatures towards the bottom of the mantle are as high as 6,700°F – and fluid, flowing at a rate of a few centimetres per year.

Core

Deep in the centre of the Earth is the Earth's core. The molten, fluid outer core, which is roughly the size of Mars, is like electrically conductive hot lava. Its flowing motion and convection currents, combined with the Earth's rotation, is what creates the Earth's magnetic field. The inner core, about the size of the Moon and made out of pure iron, is under so much pressure that it is fused solid. The core is so hot that its temperature reaches about 10,000°F – hotter than even the surface of the Sun!

LAYERS OF THE AIR

$\diamond$

THE WORD ATMOSPHERE (from the Greek *atmos* or breath, and *sphaira* or ball) refers to the gas surrounding any planet or star. Earth's atmosphere, which is held close by Earth's gravity, is made up of nitrogen, oxygen, argon, carbon dioxide, trace amounts of other gases and a small amount of water vapour – in other words, what we call 'air'. Our atmosphere provides a barrier from the sun's ultraviolet radiation and a cushion against the varying extremes of temperature from day to night. Like the inner Earth, the outer Earth also has layers, distinct areas extending above it into the invisible air, that possess their own temperatures and effects.

Troposphere

Closest to the Earth, starting anywhere from just above the Earth's surface and extending as high as 60,000 feet up, is the troposphere

(from the Greek *tropos* meaning turning or change). Most of our weather systems are contained within the troposphere, which gets colder as it extends higher up. Eighty per cent of the atmosphere's total mass is contained in this layer.

Stratosphere

This layer, from the Latin *stratus* (to stretch or extend), stretches out to about 160,000 feet above the Earth and contains the ozone layer, which is about 50,000–115,000 feet above Earth's surface. The lower part of the stratosphere possesses a near-constant temperature, but this layer of atmosphere (unlike the troposphere) increases in heat as it gets higher. Commercial aeroplanes often fly in the lowest regions of the stratosphere to avoid the turbulence and bad weather encountered in the highest reaches of the troposphere.

Mesosphere

The mesosphere (from the Greek word *mesos* or middle) extends from about 160,000 feet to 285,000 feet and is the coldest of the atmospheric layers – colder even than the lowest temperature ever recorded in Antarctica (−129°F!). This freezing layer is helpful in protecting Earth from being hit by meteors: most meteors burn up when they enter this part of Earth's atmosphere. Not much is known about the mesosphere, due to the fact that it begins just slightly higher than the maximum altitude allowed for aircraft but lower than the minimum altitude for rocketships and other space craft. Due to these limitations, the atmospheric mesosphere has not been fully explored, leading some scientists to refer to it as the 'ignorosphere'.

Thermosphere

Just above the mesosphere, the thermosphere extends from about 285,000 feet to over 400,000 feet. Named for the Greek *thermos* which means heat, the layer gets increasingly hotter as it extends farther away from the Earth. But even though it is so warm (temperatures can be as hot as 27,000°F!), it is so empty of matter that a normal thermometer would read the temperature as being way below zero. The thermosphere also contains the ionosphere, which is the part of the atmosphere ionized by solar radiation. It is also the area where auroras like the Aurora Borealis, or 'Northern Lights', are formed.

Exosphere

This uppermost region of the atmosphere extends more than 6,000 miles into space. At this level, the last level before outer space, only the lightest gases (mostly hydrogen, along with small amounts of helium, carbon dioxide and atomic oxygen) are present. The density of these molecules is so low that there is barely any chance that they will collide with each other. With no collisions holding them back, they are able to escape the Earth's gravitational pull and drift into space. The exosphere is also where many satellites orbit the Earth.

QUEENS OF THE ANCIENT WORLD III

◆

Cleopatra of Egypt: Queen of Kings

CLEOPATRA VII WAS the last of a long line of ancient Egyptian queens. She ruled Egypt for twenty-one years, from 51 to 30 BC, and was famously linked with the Roman generals Julius Caesar and Mark Antony. It was the Greek historian Plutarch (46–122 AD), however, who turned Cleopatra into a legend. Plutarch reports that although she was not conventionally beautiful, Cleopatra's persona was bewitching and irresistible. The sound of her voice brought pleasure, like an instrument of many strings, and she was intelligent, charming, witty and outrageous.

Cleopatra's City: Alexandria

Cleopatra was born in 70 BC, one of King Ptolemy XII's six children. She came of age in Alexandria, Egypt's capital city and a bustling port on the Mediterranean Sea. The Pharos Lighthouse, one of the Seven Wonders of the Ancient World, gleamed over Alexandria's harbour and welcomed ships and people to this vibrant and cosmopolitan city. The celebrated mathematician Euclid had lived there and published his thirteen-volume *Elements*, filled with all the known principles of geometry and algebra. Alexandria's marble library was the largest in the world and philosophers in the Greek tradition of Aristotle and Plato roamed Alexandria's streets.

Egypt was wealthy, besides. Craftspeople produced glass, metal, papyrus writing sheets, and cloth. The fertile countryside produced grain that was shipped all over the Mediterranean region to make bread.

Queen of a Threatened Nation

Despite this grand history, in the 50s BC, Egypt was struggling. Rome's armies had already conquered most of the nearby nations. Egypt remained independent, but no one knew how long it would be able to survive Rome's expansion. Cleopatra's father, Ptolemy XII, had made an unequal alliance with Rome. He had lost several territories, like the island of Cyprus, and faced political rebellions from his own children.

When her father died in 51 BC, Cleopatra was only eighteen years old. Still, she was named his successor, along with her twelve-year-old brother, Ptolemy XIII. Throughout her long reign, she vowed to protect Egypt's independence.

She did so until the bitter end with the help of a strong navy and her romantic alliances with the most powerful men of Rome.

Cleopatra and Julius Caesar

When Cleopatra became queen, Rome was embroiled in its own civil drama. Rome had long been a republic that prided itself on democracy and on measured rule by its Senate. Now, ambitious men were taking over. Three of these power-hungry men – Julius Caesar, Pompey and Crassus – secretly joined forces as The First Triumvirate in 60 BC to gain more control. Soon though, they began to fight each other.

In 48 BC, Julius Caesar conquered Gaul, just north of Italy. Flushed with the thrill of victory, he led his soldiers back to Rome. There was a tradition that no general's soldiers were to cross the Rubicon River into the city, but Caesar ignored that and brought his army across. He waged armed civil war against his now-enemy Pompey and the Senate, on land and at sea. Pompey fled to Alexandria, with Caesar in pursuit.

Alexandria had fallen into violence. Cleopatra and her brother were quarrelling, as each tried to steal power from the other, and there was no law and order. The sibling rulers looked to Roman rivals Pompey and Julius Caesar, knowing they needed to make an alliance but not knowing which of them they should trust.

As the fighting in Alexandria worsened, Cleopatra fled the city with her younger sister. At the same time, one of her brother's fighters, feeling emboldened, assassinated Pompey. He hoped the act would endear him to Julius Caesar, who would then take the brother's side and install him as sole Pharaoh of Egypt. However, when Caesar saw the remains of Pompey, including his signet ring with an emblem of a lion holding a sword in his paws, he was furious. Roman generals had their own sense of honour and this was no way for the life of a famed Roman leader to end. Julius Caesar was angry with the brother and banished him from Egypt.

And so in 47 BC, Cleopatra became the sole Queen of Egypt. Julius Caesar named her Pharaoh and Queen of Kings and Cleopatra styled herself as the incarnation of the Egyptian mother goddess Isis. She and Julius Caesar also fell in love. The Roman conqueror and the Egyptian queen had a child together. They named him Ptolemy Caesar, thus joining the traditional names of Egypt and Rome. His nickname was Caesarion.

Soon after Caesarion's birth, a cabal of Roman senators who feared Caesar's growing power assassinated him on the infamous Ides of March (15 March, 44 BC). Cleopatra and her son had been with Caesar in Rome and, after his death, they returned by ship to Alexandria. Having seen Roman politics up close, Cleopatra knew that Rome would play an important role in her future, but she knew not how.

Cleopatra and Mark Antony

After Caesar's death, Rome was ruled by a Second Triumvirate: Octavian, Lepidus and Mark Antony. Antony was in charge of Rome's eastern provinces and had his eye set on Egypt. In 42 BC, he summoned Cleopatra to a meeting. Cleopatra finally agreed to meet Mark Antony in the city of Tarsus. She arrived in grandeur, on a golden ship with brilliant purple sails and demanded that he come aboard and talk with her there. They too fell in love and, nine months later, she gave birth to their twins, named Alexander Helios and Cleopatra Selene II.

Mark Antony was worn out by the political life of Rome. Despite his great popularity with the Roman people, he was losing political ground to his nemesis, the brilliant Octavian. Antony moved to Alexandria to live with Cleopatra and they had another child.

Cleopatra's fate would now be inseparable from that of Mark Antony and his foe Octavian. Octavian wanted Egypt's wealth and he wanted Mark Antony's power. Julius Caesar had named Octavian his legal heir before he died, but

P. Bodart. f:

ANTONIUS et
CLEOPATRA.

Octavian still feared that Caesarion (Caesar's son with Cleopatra) would one day challenge him for the leadership of Rome.

Octavian and the Roman Senate declared war against Antony and Cleopatra. Octavian's general Agrippa captured one of Antony's Greek cities, Methone. On a September morning in 31 BC, Antony and Cleopatra commanded a flotilla of ships to arrive at the Gulf of Actium, on the western coast of Greece, to win the city back.

Egypt's Last Queen

The battle would be a disaster for Cleopatra. Before day's end she would turn her ships back to Alexandria, followed by Mark Antony, who had lost many ships and many men. Their day was over. Soon, Octavian's forces threatened Alexandria. With Antony already dead by his own hand, Cleopatra chose to kill herself rather than be taken prisoner and displayed in Octavian's triumphal march through the streets of Rome.

Still considering Caesarion a threat, Octavian had the twelve-year-old put to death. He brought Cleopatra's three children with Mark Antony to Rome, where they were raised by Octavian's sister Octavia, who had also been Antony's Roman wife and was now his widow.

QUEENS OF THE ANCIENT WORLD III: CLEOPATRA

One era ended and another began. Cleopatra was independent Egypt's last Queen and reigning Pharaoh. Having defeated Cleopatra, Octavian declared Egypt a Roman province. He commandeered Egypt's immense treasure to pay his soldiers. Having vanquished Mark Antony, Octavian ushered in the Pax Romana, or Roman Peace, and became the first Emperor of Rome.

THE FIBONACCI SEQUENCE

------◆------

THE MYSTERIOUS FIBONACCI SEQUENCE follows a deceptively simple plan. It begins with the numbers zero and 1 and thereafter each number is the sum of the two numbers before it.

The sequence looks like this: 0, 1, 1, 2, 3, 5, 8, 13, 21, 34, 55, 89, 144, 233, 377, 610, 987 and so forth.

And this is how it is made: $0 + 1 = 1$, $1 + 1 = 2$, $2 + 3 = 5$ … $34 + 55 = 89$, $55 + 89 = 144$, $89 + 144 = 233$ and so forth.

Rabbits

The origin of the Fibonacci sequence originated from an arcane question about rabbits – namely: How many rabbits would be born each month to a single male-and-female pair of rabbits, if (after the first two months, in which baby rabbits are still bunnies and cannot yet give birth) each month the original pair and every other new rabbit pair give birth to a new pair of rabbits?

Our sequence of numbers was to yield the answer, even though it didn't account for the fact that some rabbits might give birth to more than two bunnies, some bunnies might die and others might not reproduce.

But no matter. If the sequence failed to predict the real-world habits of bunnies and rabbits, it did turn out to be an intriguingly powerful set of numbers. Each number in the Fibonacci sequence, it was quickly discovered, when divided by the number directly before it, equals approximately 1.61803. The ratio became especially accurate as the numbers in the sequence got larger and larger. For instance, 8 divided by 5 equals 1.6, and 55 divided by 34 equals 1.617647058. By the time the sequence reaches 610, the number appears exactly: 610 divided by 377 is 1.61803 and 1,597 divided by 987 equals 1.61803.

The Golden Ratio

The discovery was startling because 1.61803 is the classic Golden Ratio. Also called Phi – after the sculptor Phidias, who lived during the Greek Golden Age of the fifth century, BC – the Golden Ratio shows up across the arts, in the architecture of buildings, in musical pitches and in the rhythm of poetry. The width and length of the ancient Parthenon, built in Phidias' time, followed the Golden Ratio, too, because Greek builders considered a rectangle with the sides in the ratio of 1: 1.61803 to be most pleasing to the

PHI

eye. The painter Leonardo Da Vinci called the ratio the Divine Proportion. He believed it was the ultimate key to beauty and harmony and he used it to paint the famous Mona Lisa's face.

The Golden Ratio appears throughout the natural world, too: in the centre of a daisy, a sunflower's petals and the whorl of a pinecone's scales. The spiral of a nautilus shell maps directly onto a Fibonacci rectangle. The shell's shape is an arc that becomes visible when opposing corners of the squares of a Fibonacci rectangle are connected. Because of this, the nautilus shell has been called the Golden Spiral.

Fun Fact: The Fibonacci rectangle is made like this:

* Begin by drawing one small square.

* Next to it, draw the same size square. The two squares form a rectangle.

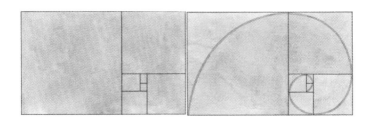

* Draw the next square using the measured length of the first rectangle's longer side; this makes the new square the sum of the two before it, as the Fibonacci sequence demands.

* Continue to draw each new square using the measure of the longer side of each prior rectangle.

The Golden Ratio of 1: 1.61803 can also be measured on the human body. The length from the belly-button to the floor and the measure of the top of the head to the floor is a Golden Ratio, and so is the relationship of the length of the hand to the combined measure of the hand and the forearm.

THE FIBONACCI SEQUENCE

Leonardo Fibonacci

The name Fibonacci comes from a medieval Italian mathematician named Leonardo of Pisa. Leonardo's father was a businessman and trader. When Leonardo was young, their family lived for many years in North Africa, in the Algerian port city now called Béjaïa. Leonardo accompanied his father to ports of call throughout the Mediterranean, from Sicily and Cyprus all the way to Syria. Some people nicknamed Leonardo 'Fibonacci' because he was the son – *Filius,* shortened to *Fi* – of the man named Bonacci, hence Fibonacci. Others called him Leonardo Bigollo, which means Leonard the traveller.

In Fibonacci's time, Europeans did maths with Roman numerals. That's the system he was taught as a young schoolboy in Italy. The problem is, with Roman numerals there is no way to perform maths operations beyond simple addition and subtraction. The Roman system doesn't even have a zero. When his family moved to North Africa, Fibonacci learned a very different way to count using Hindu-Arabic numerals, and he learned to work with decimal points and place value columns.

Intrigued by the differences between the two systems, Fibonacci wrote a book – in Latin, so that European scholars could read it – called *Liber Abaci,* which was published in the early 1200s. He described the Hindu-Arabic numerals and he wrote instructions learned from mathematicians in India about how to add, subtract, multiply and divide. This was common knowledge in the Arabic-speaking world that stretched from North Africa to the borders of India. But this kind of maths was dramatically new for Europe and changed the course of European history. Mathematicians and scholars saw the great potential in the new number and maths system, and Fibonacci became a celebrity.

There's one final twist to the story. The sequence we know as Fibonacci's was not actually discovered by Fibonacci. It was known in India as the Hemachandra numbers, named after Acharya Hemachandra, a Jain monk who was also a mathematician, a poet and a scholar and who lived from 1089 to 1173. It seems that it was Hemachandra, and not Fibonacci, who first discovered the number sequence, as part of his quest to understand the cadences of Indian poetry.

RULES OF THE GAME: HOCKEY

<hr/>

Hockey is a game we all remember from school. Played mostly in the rain, or so it seems, it's a fast-moving and energetic team sport. It's mainly played by girls at school and university level, but boys and men do play it too.

A SHORT HISTORY OF HOCKEY

Playing a game with a ball and a curved stick can be traced back to antiquity, but the game we know today dates from the nineteenth century. It was popular at English public schools and it is thought that the first rules in Britain were laid out at Eton. Different variations of the game are played throughout the world; what we play is known as Field Hockey, but other countries have adapted the game and play Ice Hockey, Roller Hockey and Road Hockey.

POSITIONS

Hockey is played by two teams made up of eleven players each.

Each team consists of the following positions, and, in a similar way to football, it is up to the players as to how many of each position they have:

* Defenders

* Midfielders

* Attackers

* Goalkeeper

EQUIPMENT

* A hockey stick – a long, curved wooden stick with a rounded section at its tip
* A small hard ball
* Shin pads. They don't look cool but they will save your legs from injury. If you don't have access to plastic shin pads, you can always compromise with pads of newspapers stuck into your long socks.

RULES OF THE GAME: HOCKEY

HOW TO PLAY

A game lasts for thirty-five minutes each way with a five-minute break at half-time. The aim of the game is to score as many goals as possible by hitting the ball past the other team's goalkeeper and into their goal. Players are permitted to tackle each other and may hit the ball with any part of the stick apart from the back, curved section.

Players may not:

* obstruct other players deliberately

* kick the ball

* make contact between their stick and another player

* raise their stick higher than shoulder height

If you hit the ball off the pitch over the sideline, play is given to the other team who can hit it from the point on the sideline where it left the pitch. If the ball is hit off the pitch over the backline, a fifteen-metre hit is awarded to the other team.

Free hits These are either five-metre hits or, as mentioned above, fifteen-metre hits. The players from the team not awarded the hit must move away from the ball by the specified distance while the other girl makes her play.

Long corner Awarded when the ball goes off the backline of the pitch, after being hit off by a defender. The attacking team may take a shot at the goal from five metres away from the corner of the pitch nearest where the ball went off.

Penalty corner Awarded against the defending team if they deliberately foul in the defending/goal area.

WORDS TO IMPRESS

STRUNK AND WHITE, in *The Elements of Style*, tell us about sesquipedalian words: 'Do not be tempted by a twenty-dollar word when there is a ten-center handy, ready and able.' But daring girls are never afraid to drop a spectacular multi-syllabic bombshell when necessary. Here are some you can use when quotidian vocabulary fails.

a **aleatoric** (EY-lee-uh-tohr-ik)
dependent on luck or a random outcome, like a roll of the dice
Aurora just laughed when doubters attributed her triumph over the pirate rogues to aleatoric influences.

b **brobdingnagian** (brob-ding-NAG-ee-uhn)
gigantic, enormous, tremendous
Lisa made constant use of her brobdingnagian vocabulary.

c **callipygian** (kal-uh-PIJ-ee-uhn)
having shapely buttocks
Jen's callipygian beauty was matched only by her strong right hook.

crepuscular (kri-PUHS-kyuh-ler)
dim; resembling or having to do with twilight
Janet's habit of planning all her best pranks to occur immediately after dinner led her mother to declare her utterly crepuscular in nature.

diaphanous (dahy-AF-uh-nuhs)
almost entirely transparent or translucent
Halloween had been a success, thought Belinda, even though little children kept bumping into her costume's diaphanous fairy wings.

echolalia (ek-oh-LEY-lee-uh)
repeating or echoing a person's speech, often in a pathological way
The baby's curious echolalia almost sounded like real conversation.

frangible (FRAN-juh-bull)
fragile; easily broken; brittle
After seeing what happened to his brothers, the third little pig resolved to build his house from a less frangible material.

frustraneous (fruhs-TREY-nee-uhs)
vain; useless; frustrating

After several frustraneous attempts, Katie gave up on trying to get her sister's attention.

g **gustatory** (GUHS-tuh-tohr-ee)
of or pertaining to taste or tasting
Rachel dug into her dinner with gustatory glee.

h **hagiology** (hag-ee-OL-uh-jee)
literature dealing with the lives of saints; a list of saints
Julie's notebook was practically a hagiology of current boy bands.

i **ineluctable** (in-ih-LUCK-tuh-bull)
inevitable, inescapable (From the Latin word *luctari*, 'to wrestle'.)
Sarah was unable to escape the ineluctable gaze of her mother.

j **jejune** (ji-JOON)
immature, uninteresting, dull; lacking nutrition
Molly resolved to use an interesting vocabulary, the better to avoid appearing jejune.

k **knurl** (nurl)
a knob, knot, or other small protuberance; one of a series of small ridges or grooves on the surface or

edge of a metal object, such as a thumbscrew, to aid in gripping

Felicity learned to rock climb by grabbing on to the knurls all the way up the wall.

languorous (LANG-ger-uhs)
lacking spirit or liveliness; dreamy; lazy
Amelia spent a languorous day by the pool.

luculent (LOO-kyoo-luhnt)
easily understood; clear or lucid
Sometimes Rebecca's homework needed to be a little more luculent.

mellifluous (muh-LIF-loo-uhs)
flowing with sweetness or honey; smooth and sweet
Anna always enjoyed chorus; she knew her voice was mellifluous.

miasma (mahy-AZ-muh)
foul vapours emitted from rotting matter; unwholesome air or atmosphere
Jemima held her nose as she passed the miasma of what her little brother referred to as 'the stinky parking garage'.

n **natalitious** (nay-tuh-LIH-shis)
pertaining to one's birthday
Mary designed elaborate invitations to announce her natalitious festivities.

nemesis (NEM-uh-sis)
a source of harm; an opponent that cannot be beaten; mythological Greek goddess of vengeance
On a good day, Christina's brother was her ally; on a bad day, he was her nemesis.

o **obsequious** (uhb-SEE-kwee-uhs)
fawning; attentive in an ingratiating manner
Eager to win her parents' approval, Vanessa was polite to the point of being obsequious.

p **persiflage** (PURR-suh-flahzh)
light banter; frivolous discussion
'We must be careful to keep our persiflage to a minimum,' Harriet whispered to Margot during class.

q **quiescence** (kwee-ES-uhns)
stillness, quietness, inactivity
Hannah revelled in the extraordinary quiescence of early morning when she awoke before anyone else.

quotidian (kwoh-TIHD-ee-uhn)
everyday, commonplace, ordinary; recurring daily
Dorothy sighed, bored by the quotidian sameness of it all.

r **rapprochement** (rap-rohsh-MAHN)
reconciliation; the re-establishing of cordial relations
After holding a grudge against him for so long, Eleanor felt it was almost a relief to have reached a rapprochement with her brother.

risible (RIZ-uh-buhl)
laughable, causing laughter
The girls knew they could always count on Polly for a risible remark.

S **sesquipedalian** (SESS-kwih-puh-DAY- lee-un)
characteristic of a long word; given to using long words
Daring girls are not shy about their sesquipedalian abilities.

sprezzatura (SPRETTS-ah-TOO-ruh)
nonchalance, effortlessness
After reading The Daring Book for Girls, *Emily was able to cartwheel with sprezzatura and verve.*

t **Truculent** (TRUCK-yuh-lunt)
pugnacious, belligerent, scathing
When Nancy was pushed too far, she became truculent.

u **ultracrepidarian** (ull-truh-krep-ih-DAIR- ee-uhn)
giving opinions or criticizing beyond one's own range of expertise
'I'd tell you what I think about your outfit, but I don't want to be all ultracrepidarian,' said Karen.

V **vitiate** (VISH-ee-ayt)
to weaken, impair, or render invalid
Penelope's debate in class vitiated Rob's argument.

W **winsome** (WIN-suhm)
sweetly or innocently charming
Holly was too busy building her treehouse to act winsome.

X **xenophobe** (ZEE-nuh-fohb)
a person who fears or hates foreigners
It was a nerve-racking moment at the picnic, when the neighbourhood xenophobe showed up with potato salad.

y **yawl** (yawl)
a ship's small boat; a yowl or howl
Helen let out a loud yawl as the boat tipped over.

Z **zaftig** (ZAHF-tik)
having a shapely figure (From the Yiddish word *zaftik*, 'juicy'.)
Bridget was proud of her strong, zaftig figure.

zeitgeist (TSIYT-giyst)
the spirit of the time; the outlook of a particular generation
Catherine was convinced the latest pop star embodied the zeitgeist of her contemporaries.

WOMEN WHO CHANGED
THE WORLD

❖

Anne Frank (1929–45)

ANNE FRANK CERTAINLY didn't mean to change the
world, and you could say that her legacy has been one of
reminding rather than changing the world. She was a normal
girl who lived in extraordinary times and, as many girls do,
she kept a record of her experiences. That diary became *The
Diary of a Young Girl* (also known as *The Diary of Anne
Frank*) and would be read by millions across the world.

Anne Frank was a young Jewish girl living in Amsterdam
with her parents, her sister Margot and her cat Moortje. On
her thirteenth birthday she received her first diary, a
treasured gift in which she would commit her thoughts, her
fears and her joys to paper. Shortly after Anne's birthday,
Margot received a demand from the Nazis to leave for a work
camp and their father, Otto, put into action the plan he had
been working on for several months. The family was to go
into hiding. Little did they realize that this hiding place would
become their home for the next two years.

Hidden at the top of a tall office building in the western
quarter of Amsterdam, the Secret Annexe (as Anne would
call it in her diary) was concealed by a large bookcase. Behind

Dit is een foto, zoals
ik me zou wensen,
altijd zo te zijn.
Dan had ik nog wel
een kans om naar
Hollywood te komen.

Anne Frank.
10 Oct. 1942

(translation)
"This is a photo as I would wish
myself to look all the time. Then
I would maybe have a chance to
come to Hollywood."
        Anne Frank, 10 Oct. 1942

that bookcase were the rooms that the Franks shared and that they would later share with four other Jews. The family was protected by friends who would bring them food and news of the war – no small feat in a country where harbouring a Jew would result in the death penalty.

Anne wrote of her life in the cramped and claustrophobic flat: her fear of discovery, her boredom at being shut away for so long, her frustration. But she also wrote of her feelings much as any other girl of her age would: how her mother irritated her, arguments with her sister, her budding feelings

of tenderness towards Peter, the son of the other family living in the Annexe. Her walls were covered in pictures of film stars, she longed to go to Hollywood, she longed to become a writer, she wondered if she would ever be married.

The diaries were never meant for public consumption. In 1944 the family was discovered by the Nazis and all the inhabitants of the Secret Annexe were sent to work camps. The only member of the family to survive was Otto Frank, and it was he who released Anne's diaries to serve as a reminder of the crimes committed against the Jews during the Holocaust.

The legacy that Anne Frank left is one that must not be forgotten. She was just one of the 6 million Jews killed during the Holocaust, but her diaries allow us to see the humanity behind the suffering. She was a normal girl, and her words speak to girls today, even after sixty years.

GREEK COLUMNS

❖

SINCE HUMAN BEINGS first moved out of caves, they've looked at their shelters and wondered how to hold the roof up. In an age long before steel beams and concrete, ancient Greek architects dreamed of creating buildings that felt perfect and sublime. To do so, they developed three orders, or systems, of columns. The three column orders were not just directions for decorating a column's capital, shaft and base, they were a vision for how all the elements of the building – the columns and the roof and the platform – would work together to build harmony, symmetry and balance.

The **Doric** order is the oldest and simplest. The capital is a circle that is topped by a square. The column shaft is either plain or fluted (fluted shafts have channelled grooves running from top to bottom). A Doric column has no base. It stands directly on the building's platform.

While Doric columns are the most austere of the three orders, the area above the columns – called the entablature – is an altogether different matter. The entablature sits over the columns and below the roof. It has three components. From bottom to top, these are the architrave, the frieze and the cornice. The first, and lowest, is the architrave, a stone beam that sits right on top of the columns. In the middle of the entablature is the frieze. The frieze is comprised of two alternating elements: the metope (pronounced me-to-pee, with the accent on the first syllable) and the triglyph. The metope is rectangular space that is decorated with carved sculptures or painted pictures. Next to it is always a triglyph, characterised by its three vertical lines. To add even more visual interest to the building, beneath each triglyph ancient Greek builders placed small guttae ('drops'). This frieze continues on all four sides of the building. Just above the frieze is the entablature's final and highest element: the cornice. This is a simple marble band or ledge. Atop the entire entablature is the pediment. This is the triangle formed by the two sloping sides of the roof and inside this triangle is even more carved sculpture. The pediment is often filled to the brim with sculptures of Greek heroes, heroines and mythological scenes.

ENTASIS

An optical illusion makes straight columns look concave and smaller at the centre. Entasis corrects this by adding a slight convex bulge along the column shaft so that the columns appear straight.

GREEK COLUMNS

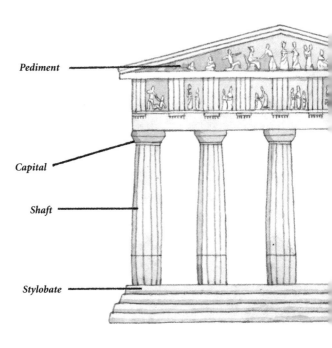

Pediment

Capital

Shaft

Stylobate

GREEK COLUMNS

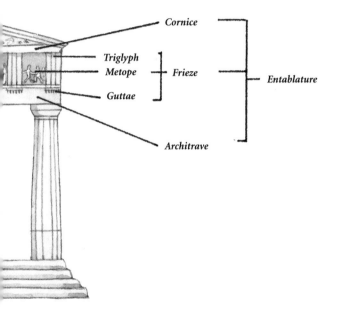

Cornice

Triglyph

Metope

Guttae

Frieze

Entablature

Architrave

GREEK COLUMNS

The **Ionic** order is more stylized. The capital has two scrolls, called volutes. Beneath these are egg-and-dart carvings or other chiselled borders. A marble band separates the capital from the column shaft. Ionic columns have shafts that are taller and more slender than those of the Doric order and they are usually fluted. The Ionic shaft rests on a base that looks like a stack of rings, and that base rests on the building's platform.

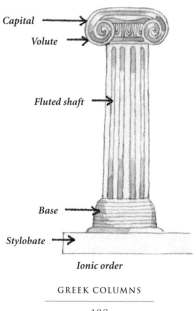

Capital ⟶

Volute ⟶

Fluted shaft ⟶

Base ⟶

Stylobate ⟶

Ionic order

GREEK COLUMNS

The **Corinthian** order developed last and it is the most elaborate. The capital has two small volute scrolls at the very top. The rest of the basket-shaped capital overflows with fancifully carved acanthus leaves, flowers, spirals and fruit. Corinthian columns have a fluted shaft and a base much like the Ionic order.

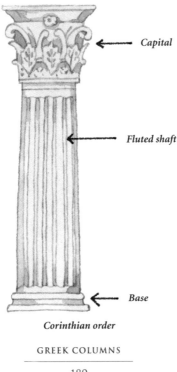

← *Capital*

← *Fluted shaft*

← *Base*

Corinthian order

GREEK COLUMNS

Fun Fact: In 333 BC, the Greek commander Alexander the Great led his armies across Asia and into India, spreading Greek culture along the way. Carved several centuries after Alexander's travels, this capital from India mixes the Greek Corinthian order with images of the Buddha.

BOYS

W ITHOUT A DOUBT you have already received many
confusing messages about what, if anything, you
should be doing with boys. Some girls are led to believe that
being liked by boys is important above all else. Some girls are
told that boys are different and that girls should adapt themselves to be like the boys they like or take care not to be too
threatening – learn about sports if a boy likes sports, or
pretend to be stupid about subjects a boy likes to excel in.
Some girls are encouraged to think of boys as protectors, or,
alternatively, as creatures that need protecting. It may seem
to some girls that suddenly boys matter a whole lot more
than they should; still others wonder what all the fuss is
about.

Many things are said of boys: Boys like sports, boys are
messy, boys don't have any feelings, boys like trucks, boys
don't like girly things, boys like to run around and eat horri-
ble food. Whatever the specific generalization, the point of
these notions about boys is to set them apart from girls as
being entirely different.

Similar statements are made about girls: Girls like pink,
girls like flowers, girls are neat and clean, girls are frivolous,
girls are emotional. Are any of these things true about

all girls? Of course not. But it's easier to think about boys and girls as being entirely different than it is to think about boys and girls as having lots of common ground.

As concerns boys themselves, you have several options. The first, of course, is to ignore them until you (and they) are nineteen. Or twenty-one. Or twenty-five.

Alternatively, you could make a boy your best friend. Boys can be excellent friends. In general, they like to do things and that makes them rather fun.

Of course a third option is romance. Some girls might be interested in this kind of thing (you will recognize them by their doodles of their name and a boy's name in a heart on their science homework); other girls might think that would be too icky to even imagine. If you are in the latter group, don't worry, you have plenty of company.

If you are in the former group, there are two main things to keep in mind. One, if a boy doesn't like you the way you are, the problem is him, not you. And two, don't try to make a boy change for you – it's important to appreciate people for who they are.

Wherever you fall on the spectrum of how you feel about boys, do treat all your friends, boys and girls, with kindness. This has gone out of fashion and that's a sad mistake.

Overall, the truth is that there's no great big mystery about boys. Boys are people and, like all people, they are complicated. And that's what makes being friends with other people interesting: you get to learn about how other people think and act and, in the process, learn a little bit more about yourself.

QUEENS OF THE ANCIENT WORLD IV

Zenobia, Queen of the East

IN THE THIRD CENTURY AD, Zenobia of Palmyra was the famed Queen of the East. According to the author of *Historia Augusta*, she had long black hair and warm brown skin, piercing dark eyes and a lyrical, strong voice. Known for her boldness, determination and fairness as a leader, she was just in her twenties when she built and ruled an empire that covered most of what is now the Middle East.

Zenobia was born around 240 AD at Palmyra, a sparkling, palm-tree-filled paradise deep in the desert of Syria (now the ruins of Tadmor, about 150 miles northeast of Damascus). Her father was a tribal ruler who had enticed her mother from Egypt to this prosperous and cosmopolitan trading outpost.

Zenobia's full given name was Iulia Aurelia Zenobia. 'Iulia' was a popular girl's name in Rome, which, even though it was far away, ruled the Syrian desert. 'Aurelia' meant that her family were Roman citizens, an important honour. 'Zenobia' came from her family's Aramaic tribe. Historians know that by the age of eighteen, she had already married the governor of Palmyra, a man named Odainat (known in Latin as

Septimius Odaenathus). Then she changed her name to Septimia Zenobia, to match his.

As wife to the land's governor, Zenobia was well educated and her court was filled with philosophers and poets. Many an evening was spent lingering over sumptuous meals, talking about Homer and Plato, making speeches and laughing at riddles and wit. The peace was disturbed in 260 AD, however, when the Persian king, Shapur, tried to take Syria from the Romans. As allies of Rome, the Palmyrans guarded the frontier where the Roman Empire met the Persian, so Odainat and Zenobia prepared for combat.

The emperor of Rome, Valerian, faced rebellion everywhere – to the west, north and now to the east. His troops were dispirited, but nonetheless he marched them to battle. The Persians had superior strength and fighting skills, so they easily routed the weary Roman soldiers. Valerian and Shapur agreed to meet at the city of Edessa and negotiate terms. When Valerian showed up, the Persians ambushed him and took him into captivity.

That's when two Roman messengers urged their horses across the desert sand to Palmyra, bringing the terrible news of Valerian's capture. Odainat and Zenobia were ready. Side by side, the couple donned armour, saddled their horses and led the army of Palmyra against the Persians, in search of Valerian.

While Odainat was a courageous and daring warrior, ancient writers tell us Zenobia was even more so, and praised her battle skills, including her exceptional way with the troops. She rallied them, kept them inspired and at times even got off her horse to march for miles with the foot soldiers. Unfortunately, the Persians killed Valerian before Odainat and Zenobia could save him, but the couple's brave leadership earned them the complete respect of the Palmyran army and people.

Was it odd for these troops to see a woman in front, her long black hair streaming out from beneath her helmet? The ancient cultures of Greece and Rome often portrayed the deity of war as a woman, and female Victory statues graced nearly every city. In fact, the Palmyran soldiers followed Zenobia to battle again and again in the following years.

In 267 AD, seven years after their first battle together, Zenobia's husband Odainat was assassinated. The royal line fell to Zenobia's toddler son, Vaballathus, who was clearly too young to rule. Zenobia, then twenty-seven years old, became queen in his stead. She dreamed of an empire of Palmyra and prepared the troops for a battle of independence.

The Romans were busy in Europe defending themselves from the Goths, Zenobia knew, so she attacked the Roman province of Egypt. The Egyptians, too, were distracted, off battling pirates in the Mediterranean Sea. She conquered them and then went to conquer cities in Arabia, Palestine and Syria. By 269 AD, she declared her empire's independence from Rome and minted new coins with her image and the word 'REGINA' – Queen.

Historians tell us that Zenobia ruled tolerantly as Queen of the East, drawing on the Palmyran traditions of hospitality and openness to treat all people with fairness, including the pagans, Jews and Christians of her empire. She opened new trade routes and met Christian bishops and other leaders of the cities she conquered.

As Zenobia expanded her Palmyran empire, armies threatened the larger Roman Empire on all sides. The new Roman emperor, Aurelian, was battling the Goth and Visigoth tribes in northern Europe. When his messengers arrived with news of Queen Zenobia's expanding kingdom, Aurelian set off for Egypt, determined to win the territory back, and then to Turkey (which in ancient times was called Asia Minor). After these small victories, he prepared to attack Antioch, a city in northern Syria that Zenobia now ruled.

Zenobia had never faced the vast legions of the mighty Roman army. She could have given up and returned to the Roman fold, but decided instead to take a last stand and save the heart of her hard-earned empire. She assembled the troops along one side of the north-flowing Orontes

QUEENS OF THE ANCIENT WORLD IV: ZENOBIA

River. Her soldiers fought all day, Zenobia along with them. Then, as the sun dipped towards the western horizon, the tired soldiers, bleary and water-starved after a long day, fell into a trap, in which the Romans massacred them from all sides.

Zenobia managed to escape with seventy thousand soldiers and retreated to the city of Emesa. They found a hill and, under cover of night, climbed to the top and lay in wait, ready to rain down arrows on the Roman soldiers. The Romans, though, pulled out their colourful shields, held high overhead, each shield meeting the next to cover the men and protect them from the Palmyrans' arrows and darts. In this formation, the Romans pushed forward up the hill. When they reached the Palmyran marksmen, they moved their shields forward and down and attacked.

Thousands of troops died on the battlefield. Zenobia herself barely escaped and even her trusted horse fell in the battle. She commandeered a camel and turned the slow beast towards the sandy hinterlands of the Syrian desert, with hopes that the plodding animal could take her one hundred miles east to Persia, where she would be safe from Rome.

'I promise you life if you surrender,' Aurelian wrote to her. Zenobia had other plans, but it was Aurelian's turn for victory. He laid siege to her beloved Palmyra and sent his best soldiers on horseback to capture the fallen paradise's fugitive queen. As she neared the Euphrates River, so close to freedom, the emperor's horsemen reached Zenobia and captured her.

The remainder of Zenobia's life is shrouded in myth. Where one ancient historian reports that she died in captivity, another writes that Aurelian took her to Rome. It is said that in 274 AD, Zenobia was wrapped in chains of gold and made to walk down Rome's main boulevard as Aurelian celebrated his triumph over the many tribes he had battled. Still another tale suggests that some time later, Zenobia was released. In her absence, Palmyra had rebelled against Rome once more and had been crushed. Some tales hold that, with no home to return to, Zenobia lived the rest of her life not far from Rome, in Tivoli.

RULES OF THE GAME: LACROSSE

WE OFTEN THINK of lacrosse as a sport played and originated in British public schools, but in fact it was first played by native North Americans as far back as the fifteenth century. It came to the UK in the nineteenth century, and has been played here ever since.

EQUIPMENT

Lacrosse is played with a crosse: a wooden stick with a net at the end which is used to catch and throw the ball between players.

TEAM

A lacrosse team is made up of twelve players: normally five attackers, six defenders and a goalkeeper.

HOW TO PLAY

The game is played in two halves of thirty minutes each way on a pitch made up of a goal at either end with two restraining lines and a centre section. The aim of the game is to score goals by throwing the ball into your opponents' goal.

Play starts at the centre point as a member from each team crosses sticks and a ball is thrown into the air. The first girl to catch it gets possession of the ball. If you catch the ball, you may run with it in your crosse or pass it to another player in your team. Your opponents will try to take control of the ball either by intercepting it during a throw or by trying to dislodge it from your crosse. This is called a 'check' and the player performing the check must be in front of the player with the ball and must not lean across her to try to tap the ball out of her crosse.

If the ball is thrown out of the boundary of the pitch, the player closest to it when it went out is given possession.

The restraining line at each end of the pitch marks off the area where only seven attackers and eight defenders are allowed at any one time. Within this area is a semicircle in front of the goal where players must keep at least one stick-length away from each other.

FOULS

There are two types of foul: major and minor.

Major fouls include blocking another player, slashing at another player with your crosse, charging into or at another player, throwing a ball in a dangerous or uncontrolled way, and obstructing another player.

Minor fouls include using your body to hit the ball for your own advantage, using your hand to ward off another player, checking a player who doesn't have the ball in her crosse, and fouling in the goal area.

The penalty for fouls is a free position for the player fouled against. Major fouls result in the offending player having to stand four metres behind the girl with the free position while she is allowed to take the ball. Minor fouls result in the offender having to stand four metres off from the girl with the free position, in the direction that she came from when she committed the foul.

GAMES FOR A RAINY DAY

◆

THERE ALWAYS SEEM to be too many of those days when the weather is too bad to go outside and you are doomed to spend the day watching raindrops race each other down the outside of the window. Staying inside is never going to be as fun as being outside with the wind in your hair and the world at your fingertips, but here are a few ideas to pass the time more quickly until the sun comes out.

Board games

Normally kept stacked inside a cupboard waiting for Christmas, board games are a great way of passing a rainy day. Old favourites such as Monopoly, Cluedo, and Snakes and Ladders can last for hours and are good fun, too. But even better is making your own board game.

HOW TO MAKE A BOARD GAME

* Start off with some stiff cardboard, with white paper glued onto it to create a board.

* Using your imagination, create a scene for your board. We suggest using the format of an existing board game – take Snakes and Ladders for example – and adapting it. Mark off squares in a sequence, decorating along the way.

* Now you need to create scenarios for each player to do as they land on a square. These can be fun and physical: 'You've landed a job testing space hoppers. Jump thirty times on your space hopper to show you can do the job,' or more quiz-based: 'You have landed on a Brain Square. Name the capital of Canada.' Have fun coming up with challenges and questions to fox your friends.

* Make sure you decide on the rules before you play – you don't want to give your brother a chance to cheat!

Card games

If you've played all the card games you know and it's still raining, how about a game of Patience?

RULES OF THE GAME

Patience is a game for one person.

Start by setting out the cards in preparation: from the left, place one card facing up in front of you and then a row of six cards facing down. Then place another card facing up on top of the first concealed card, and then five cards facing down on top of the cards already laid out. Continue until you have seven cards facing up, each with a growing pile of cards facing down underneath them. You'll have a few leftover cards which you will deal from.

The aim of the game is to create four straight suits from King down to Ace, in alternating colours. You can move whole runs from one column to another. If you have a space left by moving one card from one column to another, this can be filled with a King.

Aces can be kept to one side and used as a piling station for other cards of the same suit – but only in numerical order, so only a Two of Clubs can go on top of an Ace of Clubs, followed by a Three of Clubs and so on.

Use the cards in your hand to help you move, turning them over three at a time and moving them into columns as and when you can. You should aim to release the cards from under the piles by moving the cards on top of them; as soon as a face-down card is revealed, you can turn it over and start a new column with it.

Good luck – and have patience.

Putting on a play

Putting on a play for your friends and family can be really good fun. It gives you a chance to be really creative and to show what a great actor you are.

You can choose a play that already exists and use it to work from. Even better, though, is to come up with your own story or to act out one of your favourite books. Decide who will play which part (you might want to bagsy the most exciting, attractive or interesting character for yourself, of course!) and improvise from there. Think about their personalities, their likes, their dislikes, their relationships with the other characters.

Designing the set can also be a lot of fun. If you are holding it in your living room or even in your garden, you can devise a backdrop to show any setting you like. Make use of any props you find around the house. Raid dressing-up boxes, kitchen cupboards and airing cupboards for props – the more flamboyant, the better!

When it comes to the moment of revealing the play, your family sitting waiting expectantly, remember to take a deep breath, forget those nerves and break a leg!

Charades

Charades is a good old-fashioned parlour game that is still fun to play today. One person is the actor and has to think up something – a book title, a person, a thing, anything – that they will act out, and no words are allowed. It is up to everyone else to guess what they are acting out.

Here are a few tips to get you started:

Show what type of thing it is by starting off with one of the following:

* Film – imitate an old cine camera by circling your hand near the side of your head.
* Book – open your palms out, like a book.
* TV show – draw a rectangle, TV shape, in the air.
* Person – stand with your hands on your hips.
* Quotation – make quotation marks in the air with your fingers.

Everyone else should shout out until they have the right answer. Show them they are right by nodding or point at your nose to indicate that they are 'spot on'.

Show the number of words by raising the appropriate number of fingers in the air.

Show which word you are acting out by raising the appropriate finger, i.e. your first finger if it is the first word.

If the words have more than one syllable, show this by placing the appropriate number of fingers together on your left arm with your right hand.

Show you are acting out something that sounds like your word by cupping your ear with your hand.

After that, use your imagination!

ILLUSTRATIONS

Illustrations on pp i, 20, 24, 27, 28, 39, 44, 46, 52, 95, 103, 163, 186–90 © Alexis Seabrook

Illustrations on pp 15, 125–30, 168–9, 203 © Joy Gosney, 2008

Andrea Buchanan and Miriam Peskowitz

The Pocket
DARING
Book
for
Girls
Adventures & Pursuits

The Daring Book for Girls

Andrea Buchanan and Miriam Peskowitz

I have learnt all
about hukius, pirats and
mop

HCR